The Performer's Guide to the Collaborative Process

Sheila
Kerrigan

Heinemann
Portsmouth, NH

792

Heinemann
A division of Reed Elsevier Inc.
361 Hanover Street
Portsmouth, NH 03801–3912
www.heinemanndrama.com

Offices and agents throughout the world

© 2001 by Sheila Kerrigan

The author and publisher wish to thank those who have generously given permission to reprint borrowed material:

Figure 5–2 is adapted from *On Conflict and Consensus* by C. T. Lawrence Butler and Amy Rothstein. Food Not Bombs Publishing, Portland, ME, 1991.

Library of Congress Cataloging-in-Publication Data
Kerrigan, Sheila.
    The performer's guide to the collaborative process / Sheila Kerrigan.
        p.   cm.
    Includes bibliographical references and index.
    ISBN 0-325-00311-4
    1. Drama—Technique.   2. Playwriting.   3. Improvisation (Acting).
I. Title.
PN1661 .K475   2000
792—dc21

                                                                00-058163

Editor: Lisa A. Barnett
Production: Lynne Reed
Cover design: Joni Doherty
Manufacturing: Deanna Richardson

Printed in the United States of America on acid-free paper
05   04   DA   3   4   5

◼️**C**ontents

List of Illustrations   vii

Acknowledgments   ix

Introduction   xi

Part 1: Creative Processes   1

1   Getting Started: How to Get an Idea
    for a Performance Piece   3

2   The Next Step: How to Generate
    Material About Your Idea and How
    to Begin to Shape It   28

3   Deepening the Work: The One-Element-at-
    a-Time Creative Process   45

4   Organizing Your Material, Getting Stuck,
    and Cutting   69

Part 2: Collaborative Processes   83

5   Structuring Safety, Time, Power,
    and Decision Making   85

6   Group Dynamics: What We Need in Groups,
    Ways We Get Power, Roles We Play,
    How Groups Behave   106

7   Communicating Well in Groups:
    Peaceful Communication, Constructive
    Critiques, Conflict Resolution   123

Appendix A: Games and Exercises   153

Appendix B: People I Interviewed   155

Bibliography   161

Index   167

List of Illustrations

Figure		Page
1–1	Tony Montanaro in *Baseball*	4
3–1	C. W. Metcalf	46
3–2	The Web of Compositional Elements	48
3–3	The Central Elements of Composition	49
3–4	Laurie Wolf, Jef, and Sheila Kerrigan in TOUCH Mime Theater's *Just One of Those Days*	50
4–1	Steven Kent	70
4–2	Page from *Just One of Those Days* binder	72
5–1	Consensus Decision-Making Flow Chart	100

Acknowledgments

It is a privilege to acknowledge the more than seventy creative people who generously gave of their time and shared their wisdom and experience in interviews with me. Their contributions enlighten every page. I thank my parents, James J. and Margaret M. Kerrigan, and my teachers: William Lawrence Bockius, who told me I can write; Alan Cheuse, who taught me how; C. W. Metcalf, who revealed the joys of collaboration and helped me trust in the creative process; and Tony Montanaro, who invented valuable creative tools. Thanks to Ellen E. M. Roberts for editing these pages and for giving me her support; to Steve Durland for his fine graphics; and to Paula Larke and Alice Loyd for their timely help with the manuscript. Thanks to Jef, for twenty-five years of happy collaboration. And my deepest gratitude goes to Steve Clarke, for his faith, his photos, his love, and his constant support through hurricane, performance, and manuscript preparation.

■𝒜ntroduction

This book is for anyone who wants to work with a group and invent a performance or for anyone who works in a group and wonders if there are better ways to work together. It is for dance, mime, and drama students and teachers and for amateur and professional performers, directors, choreographers, and playwrights. It is for drama teachers who can't find scripts suitable for their classes, and for dance teachers who want their students to choreograph their own dances.

It is a practical guide to creating original performances collaboratively that is based on interviews and workshops with performing artists, cohousing architects, playwrights, group therapists, computer designers, site sculptors, muralists, team builders, and peacemakers; on research in group dynamics, communication, and conflict; on my studies of performing arts; and on my seventeen years in a collaborative company called TOUCH Mime Theater.

Starting with how to come up with an idea for a piece, Part 1 examines various ways to research and generate material, to shape and organize material, and to keep moving forward with the work. Part 2 explores working in groups and shows how to create safety, build trust, share power, make decisions openly, and communicate skillfully, including constructive criticism, and peaceful conflict resolution.

Why Work Collaboratively?

The collaborative creative process is such fun for me that I marvel that I get paid to do it. Entering an empty studio at the beginning of a writing session thrills me. Playing off others' ideas delights me and spurs me to invent things I never would find alone. The expansion of creativity is like an atomic chain reaction. Ideas carom off each other, flying in new directions or fusing to create wildly original concepts.

Dive In!

Whether you have been collaborating for years or are just beginning, you can use this book as a springboard. You will find approaches to various stages of the creative process from over seventy collaborative artists. You will discover ways to maintain a healthy group and deal with problems in group dynamics from the standpoint of psychology, sociology, business communication, and peace building. I invite you to jump into the excitement of collaborative creativity, in the hope that you will experience the intense joy it has brought me.

The Performer's Guide to the Collaborative Process

CREATIVE PROCESSES

Getting Started

How to Get an Idea for a Performance Piece

If You Have No Idea: Don't Panic! Do Something

Most artists experience fear when starting a new project, but they start working anyway. Fear is an emotion; you can work while you feel it.

Tony Montanaro, who started performing in the 1950s and who has taught performance arts at the Celebration Barn in Maine since 1972, said he never gets ideas out of the blue. His ideas come from the studio—either from seeing what someone else has done, or from seeing what he has done. He has recently taken up etching. He described how he starts a new monotype, and though he talked about moving paint across a plate, the same process applies to moving the body through time and space in the rehearsal studio.

> I'll make a movement with paint across the plate, and look at it. Suddenly it will suggest something, and that will go somewhere else, and I just keep finding what it suggests, but I'm one inch behind it. I let the spirit move me, frankly, and my body follows it. . . . I trust that there will be inspiration. Once the movement begins, I trust it. Everybody should trust it.
>
> Because, it's true, everybody knows what to do *after* they get going. You *know* what to do next. You don't know what to do *first*. It takes courage to say, "Well here goes blue! Splat." You throw it

Figure 1–1. Tony Montanaro in Baseball. *Photograph by C. C. Church, courtesy of Tony Montanaro.*

out there. A lot of people don't know what to do with their first move, they figure they're going to fail before they even start. They're afraid to make that first gesture.

Bill Allard, of Duck's Breath Mystery Theater, a five-man comedy troupe in San Francisco, related how they start writing a new show. They usually know the title before they start writing:

Everybody is so grumpy about having to start to do it. Nobody wants to start. The beginning of rehearsal is such a drag. . . . We'd start when somebody would say, "We're working on *MacScout*." Then there'd be this dead silence. Everybody's really grouchy.

Fear hits many artists when they begin a new work—fear of failure, of success, or of the unknown. Some people fear that their idea is no good. But an idea is simply a starting point. It is not responsible for the end product. If you explore your idea with an open mind, you will find something interesting. To escape the fear of starting, start.

Try, Fail, Try, Fail

Failures are an important part of the creative process. Love your failures, embrace them, learn from them.

Hardin Minor, who, with Eddie Williams, cofounded OMIMEO Mime Theatre in Charlotte, North Carolina, talked enthusiastically about their first rehearsals for a new piece. In contrast to Duck's Breath's glumness, Minor and Williams excitedly throw ideas back and forth until one says, "Let's try this." Then they jump into an improvisation. Minor said,

> It's a give-and-take process. . . . We still rely a great deal on the chaos of the moment—the inspired improvisational experience. I love that. It's fortunate when you find someone that you correspond with internally—when Eddie goes up, I go down. . . . It's a process of trying and failing, trying and failing, and finding little bits within each failure that then add up to a solution.

They embrace failures because they trust that the try-fail cycle will generate material. All the artists I spoke with share this trust in the process.

Where You Start Isn't Where You'll End Up

The creative process includes chance happenings. A discovery in rehearsal can shift your direction. Mistakes turn out to be gems. Babs Davy of the Five Lesbian Brothers, a comedy theater group that emerged from the WOW Café in New York, marveled that when they set out to write a musical, titled *Seven Brides for Five Brothers*, they didn't come up with any music. When they set out to write a comedy about secretaries, they ended up with dark stories of self-destruction. Rather than hanging on to their starting idea, they followed the flow of rehearsal to a new place.

Play Games to Warm Up

Studies show that people who have been joking and laughing think more creatively than those who have not.[1]

One way to overcome the fear of starting is to play silly games to warm up. A playful attitude—curiosity, a child-like openness to experimentation, and a delight in surprises—is a creative attitude. Playing builds rapport, explores possibilities, stimulates creativity, fosters safety, allows for risk taking, encourages spontaneity, releases aggression, and awakens us to the moment. Play nurtures an intimate and healthy relationship with failure.

Play any game, as long as it's fun. Run around tossing and catching balls. Play tag or keep-away or basketball with your own rules. Tell jokes. Here is a game that wakes up creative thinking.

Protean Catch

This is a classic game for two or more. One person shows an imaginary ball of a certain size, weight, and texture. She passes it with a certain speed and direction to someone in the circle. The receiver accepts the same ball with the same size, weight, texture, speed, and direction. He plays with it briefly. Then he changes some quality about it and passes it to someone else. Each catcher receives what was passed, plays with it briefly, makes a specific change, and passes the new object in a specific manner.

For example, if the initiator shows a marble and shoots it with his thumb across the circle, the receiver can stop it, shoot it, and change it to a ring. She might put it on her finger, show it to her neighbor, remove it, and place it on her neighbor's finger. Her neighbor could take it off, and change it into a heavy lump. He might drag it and heave it into the next player's hands. She could drag it around, and transform it into a barbell.

This process—accepting whatever a partner sends you, replying by changing it, and sending it back out—forms a building block of improvisational development. This game encourages players to grab whatever idea pops into their heads and run with it. The key lies in focusing on the object. You are focused on it when it tells you how it wants to change, and you follow the impulse it gives you. This feels different from deciding what you are going to do and doing it. Giving the object your focus brings it to life: the object will speak to your body and ideas will spring up freely.

Variation: when the initiator shows an object, the next player joins the initiator somehow, either using the same object or doing a related activity. When they finish, the initiator pulls out. The person remaining (the new initiator) shows a new object. As soon as the next person recognizes it, she joins in with a related activity. They interact, then the initiator pulls out.

If the initiator plays what looks like a jazz saxophone, someone can join in by playing another instrument, listening while sipping a drink, dancing, dropping money into a hat, conducting, or many other choices. Eventually, more than one person can join in and a scene can develop. Starting with a simple object and creating a sense of place by adding people engaged in related activities, each player can develop a character.

Where the Ideas Are

Ideas are everywhere. All you have to do is pick one. Don't judge it; explore it.

Bill Allard explained that at Duck's Breath they stopped worrying about the quality of their initial idea:

> I don't think in general people would say, "Here's an idea that's funny or good." In general, ideas are just ideas, and then it's your job to make it interesting or funny. . . . We did any idea we had. It's not a *good* idea so much as an *idea!*
>
> When we were writing a western, the idea was to do a western. . . . Merle [Kessler] did an outline for it. Everybody figured out their character and came to [the] writing session dressed as their character for a few days. Once you decide you're going to do it, you start making it go.

Early on, he recalled, they went through "the naysayer period," but it didn't last, because they realized that—especially at the beginning

—all ideas have value. They got in the habit of saying, "Yeah! Great idea! Good! Good!"

> You don't have to pooh-pooh a bad idea at first, because it will die its own death later on, and the guy who thought of it will know it doesn't fit. Even some great ideas will get thrown out, because the great idea has to be a part of a scene's needs. . . . The key was not to negate the idea. Somehow we would use the idea elsewhere.

In choosing an idea, don't look for the most original thought since the big bang. Don't wait for an idea so funny you writhe on the floor hooting. Your idea is just a starting point; it can be mundane. Much of creativity lies in seeing what you look at, listening to what you hear, sensing what you feel, asking questions, and playing.

Before cofounding AwarenessAct—a New York ensemble that performs for teens—Diana Gore attended college on the East Coast. At a conference on the West Coast, she noticed that the graffiti in the women's rooms treated the same themes as graffiti back East. She started copying graffiti, then collaborated with a group of women to create a piece based on bathroom graffiti.

Many great performances treat ordinary stuff. Bill Cosby transformed the ancient story of Noah's Ark into a comedy routine that made him famous. Lily Tomlin centered *The Search for Intelligent Life* on a street person and Campbell's soup. Blue Man Group's show involves drumming, eating, eliminating, and making messes.

You don't need an original, brilliant, deep idea to create an original, brilliant, deep performance. What you do with your idea, how deeply you explore it, and what kind of twist you give it are all more important than where you start.

Pick an idea that sparks several more ideas, something that moves you and gives a physical jolt or soft caress to your feelings. Listen for the idea that resonates with your experience. If it piques your curiosity, go with it.

What follows are twenty-two ways to find an idea for a new piece. Pick one or two and try them a few times. If you don't discover an idea that intrigues you, try another way. Once you choose an idea, you can research it by using any of the other twenty-two ways, or you can skip to the next chapter, which explains how to start generating material for your idea.

Twenty-Two Ways to Find an Idea for a Piece

1. Rounds

Rounds are brainstorming sessions for performers. They generate a lot of ideas quickly, and can boost a group's excitement for a new work.

Tony Montanaro invented rounds for his students as a way to control unchecked egos, let everyone contribute, and allow people to spark each other's creativity.[2]

Rounds have rules: First, everyone agrees on a topic; for example, a broad topic like the ocean, circles, or religion. Or, you can do a round with an object, like a mask. Later on in the process, you can use a round to attack a specific problem: "How can we create the atmosphere of a city street?" "How can we segue from this section to the next?" If you don't have a topic, you can do an open round.

Second, everyone takes turns. When your turn comes, you quickly get on stage, do a short, half-baked idea on the topic (if there is one), and sit back down. You don't try to succeed or produce something slick or clever. If you have an idea and you don't know if you can convey it, you do it anyway. If you need help from others, you quickly draft them, sketch for them what they should do, and do it together.

If you choose the ocean as a topic, any actions or impressions of any aspect of ocean or beach would be appropriate; for instance, lying down on your stomach and not moving, undulating, rocking back and forth slowly, making whooshing sounds while darting around, drafting several people to make fishlike movements with hands and feet, dive-rolling across the floor, or singing a sea chantey.

It doesn't matter if anyone understands what you do; that's not the point. The point is to stimulate others' creativity. Sometimes the abstract, weird turns give the best jolt to creative thought.

Third, no talking is allowed, except on stage. Don't comment, question, applaud, or make faces.

Fourth, as soon as you finish your turn, the next person gets up quickly, does their half-baked idea, and sits down. Then the next, and the next. No one passes up a turn. If you don't have an idea when your turn comes, get up and do what somebody else did in your own way. Keep going around until people run out of ideas, or until the quality of the ideas slides downhill.

Fifth, once you declare the round over, you talk: you say what you saw that you liked; ideas that you got from watching; where something you saw might go; how some parts might connect. You don't talk about anything you yourself did. You don't question or criticize—overtly or covertly—anything anyone did.

When beginners do rounds, they tend to focus on their own ideas. "What will I do when my turn comes? Was my idea good?" You will get the most creative results, however, when you focus on what others do. Let someone else's idea tickle your mind, and you will surprise yourself with ideas that wouldn't have occurred to you on your own. Therein lies the joy of collaboration.

We used rounds in TOUCH when we first started work on a new piece, on whatever aspects we knew anything about. The rounds generated material we could start putting together. We also used rounds when we didn't know how to proceed. The round bridged the gap between where we stood and where we wanted to go. We would define a problem and do a round on it: "We want tango music here; let's do a round on tango moves."

Because rounds generate many ideas quickly, it is helpful to take notes. As always in the creative process, many ideas are bland by themselves, but you need all of them to find the spicy ones. The bland ones go in the garbage heap; the spicy ones go into the pile of useful material.

After you discuss the round, you might have enough material to put together a short, temporary sequence. Go ahead; try it out, fiddle with it. Write it down or learn it. You've already taken the first step.

2. Brainstorms

Brainstorming can also generate ideas. To brainstorm, everyone agrees on a topic, question, or problem, and calls out ideas on it. Scribes write the ideas without editing on a chalkboard or big piece of paper. No one evaluates or questions any ideas. Participants listen open-mindedly, allow other ideas to jiggle their own, piggyback their ideas onto someone else's, or link ideas they see as related. The session continues until everyone runs out of ideas.

Then participants evaluate the ideas by talking positively about what might work, what has potential. You can ask clarifying questions, but if the person whose idea you question does not have the answers, that's OK. You can add onto someone's idea and discuss it further. You can bring up negative aspects only in terms of reformulating the idea, for instance, "I like the image of a thousand baby dolls dropping from the sky, but it will cost a lot. Can we get the same effect for less money?"

Studies have found that since the group free-for-all tends to inhibit unassertive people and interrupt thinking for others, some of the best ideas never make it onto the list in a brainstorming session.[3] According to these studies, brainstorms work best in groups of five.

Nominal Group Technique

An alternative method, called nominal group technique, allows people who work best alone to dredge up more ideas.

In nominal group technique, everyone agrees on a problem or topic, then brainstorms silently on paper. I use a long piece of butcher paper tacked to the wall and give everyone different-colored markers. Everyone writes any and all of their ideas on the wall. Then they silently read all the other ideas, checking off any that hold interest for them and adding any more they think of to their own list.

After all the ideas are on paper, each person can explain his own ideas to the group, without critiques or evaluations. You can follow up with rounds on any ideas people want to try out, then have a round-table discussion about how to expand or consolidate the ideas that prove interesting. Only discuss how things might work, not what won't work.

3. Impulse Exercises

An impulse is an idea, image, inner voice, feeling, or physical urge that you embody and vocalize fully.

Tony Montanaro teaches impulse exercises as a way to research a topic. If you don't have a topic, you can do an open impulse exercise on whatever comes up. The group agrees on a theme and a time limit—from two to five minutes. One person or several can work at a time. Beginners should stick with solo impulse exercises. If more than one person participates, they can either ignore each other and work as if alone or pay attention to each other and get impulses from within and from the others. Somebody must watch.

The players close their eyes, breathe, and relax. When they are ready, an observer names the topic and the participants begin.

Using the topic as a mantra, each person does whatever comes into her mind the moment it occurs, and stays with it until another idea pops up. At that moment, she abandons the initial impulse, and enacts the new one. She commits totally to the current impulse while staying open to any new impulses that flit by. Some impulses come with a big bang, but many come in a tiny whisper, which might get drowned out by exclusive attention to the present impulse. This process continues until the observer calls time.

If I pick sugar as my topic, my first impulse might come from an image of a bowl of white, granulated sugar. I respond by making a bowl shape with my body. I envision a sugar cube, so I move in straight lines and 90-degree angles. I see sugar pouring: I fall and slide and make a shushing sound. I remember a book about harvesting cane. I slash with a machete, sing a work song, stop for a cool drink. Hypoglycemia pops up next: I make exploding movements, enact a sugar buzz, and crash. I cycle through sugar melting in a cup of coffee, a vat of steaming maple sap, the stickiness of wet sugar, the shininess of granules—whatever images, sounds, words, tastes, or smells crowd into my head.

With each new impulse, I abandon the previous one. Some impulses last two seconds; some longer. I don't delve deeply into any; I'm going for quantity. Impulse exercises hand the observers a slew of experimental ideas on the topic.

When time runs out, observers and players switch places. Nobody comments until everyone has done the exercise. Then discussion follows: what was appealing, what got you, what you thought of, and how you might use it.

4. Harangues
Harangues address the problem of the lack of confidence and the consequent lack of commitment to the moment on stage.

I learned harangues from Tony Montanaro.[4] A harangue is a solo, open improvisation where you get to say and do whatever you want until time runs out. Sometimes it becomes a wild rant. You spend a minute breathing, relaxing, and emptying the mind of chatter. At a signal from a viewer, you begin. You talk and move rapidly and continuously for several minutes—saying and doing whatever pops into your imagination. You grab the smallest impulses and follow them to the hilt. You might get an impulse from something you see, hear, feel, smell, touch, or imagine. If your first impulse comes from a fluttery feeling in your stomach, follow that. You might double over clutching your stomach and moaning. You might then want to go to the hospital, so there you go. Or you might next hear a noise that frightens you, so you hide, still doubled over, moaning in a whisper.

While totally engaged in your action, you remain open to other impulses, allowing them to affect you. You keep adding incoming impulses to what you have already done. You play to your fullest extent—you take every emotion, every objective, every action to its furthest logical conclusion. You commit yourself wholeheartedly to the moment.

When people first practice harangues, they become self-indulgent because they release emotions they have been bottling up. After they break through their need for emotional release, the harangues grow more interesting. Harangues can be hilarious, nerve-wracking, disgusting, or scary. Harangues help performers practice the power of total commitment to the moment. They dig up material that otherwise might not escape the censors in our minds, and that can plant the seed of a new piece.

5. Statues and Evolving Statues

Statues are a way of thinking physically.

Tony Montanaro uses statues as a group improvisational laboratory.[5] In statues, a group stands on the boards, ready. The observer gives them a topic, the Civil War, for example. They let the topic sink in for a few seconds, and then they all form one statue of that topic. They don't discuss it. Each person pays attention to the other statue members, the space between them, their relative weight, and their relationships. They work together to express the Civil War with one still image. They hold it until the observer signals them to let go.

To evolve the statue, they make a series of statues all on the topic. They move when the observer signals them. They take the statue to the next step. They freeze when they feel they have achieved the next statue, or when the observer signals them. When the observer signals, they move again. They work together, each member fitting in and contributing to the whole. Evolving statues can turn into one slow-motion, constantly changing statue.

Random Statues

Random statues open the actors' imaginations to possibilities that arise from a combination of external and internal stimuli.

Barbara Vann worked with The Open Theatre in the 1960s and later became coartistic director of Medicine Show Theatre Ensemble in New York. She described random statues: One person watches while the others move around the space. When the watcher signals, each actor places himself in relation to someone else in a still pose. While there, he imagines what could be happening in this relationship. At another signal, they break up and move again. At the next signal, they get into a new relationship with someone, and imagine what's going on. They repeat several times.

Then the watcher reflects to the actors what she perceives to be the content of their actions. The watcher might come out with, "It's about power, or a family."

The actors don't need to say what they imagine in the relationships, although they can when they finish. They may afterward improvise on an interesting relationship or series of relationships.

6. Improvisations

Dominique Dibbell of Five Lesbian Brothers said her company uses Viola Spolin's book, *Improvisation for the Theater:*

> We work with improvisation a lot. At first it was a way of establishing a basis of trust, a way of opening up on a nonverbal plane. We use different types of theater games, like [Viola] Spolin's: . . . We'll write down on different slips of paper a time, a place, a character, and a quality, and pick one from each category, and improvise, just duets or trios, incorporating all the elements. It's just basic stuff, games, to get us moving and aware of each other.

Babs Davy, another of the Lesbian Brothers, added,

> We like to warm up first with nonverbal improvs, to gain trust. They slow you down. They get you moving in space. They force you to focus on action instead of thoughts. Then we gradually add words into silent improvs. Sometimes we pick one word, . . . so each person has only one word to use in an improv.

In addition to Spolin, Keith Johnstone, Daniel Nagrin, Tony Montanaro, and Lynda Belt and Rebecca Stockley have written about improvisation games and exercises.[6]

7. Energy Work

C. W. Metcalf studied with Yass Hakoshima, a Japanese mime who taught technique in terms of body energy. Metcalf taught the members of TOUCH. We practiced energy exercises daily and found many ideas for new works.

Energy flows through our bodies along pathways called meridians, and our bodies create energy fields that surround us like an envelope, or bubble.[7] Energy work involves releasing tension, increasing energy flow, and charging your energy field with the breath. Once you can feel your energy flow, you can connect different parts of your body, letting one hand push the other without skin-to-skin contact, for example. If you establish a strong energy flow, you can create palpable invisible objects in space. Then you can sense someone else's energy field, and establish an energy connection with a partner.

Energy exercises ask you to become aware of your body: the breath; the skin; minute movements within the body; sensations of heat, color, or tingling in the area just beyond the skin.[8]

Energy Basics

Focusing all your attention on your breath and the myriad sensations of the body stills the mind's chatter and allows creative impulses to arise.

Close your eyes and breathe deeply. Pay attention to the parts of your body touched by your breath. Feel the air moving from the tip of your nose, into your sinuses, throat, bronchia, and lungs. Feel your rib cage expanding and releasing. Feel how your shoulders, neck, and head float above the breath. Feel your diaphragm pushing into your belly and the bowl of your pelvis. Feel the muscles of your back, buttocks, and thighs as they adjust to the breath.

Imagine that each inhalation fills your body with light and energy, while each exhalation empties your body of tension. Imagine the breath going directly into your abdomen, filling your belly with light, and releasing any unneeded tension as you exhale. Next, imagine the breath filling the bowl of your pelvis with light and energy, and cleansing it of unneeded tension. Go through each part of your body, filling each part with light and energy with your inhalation, emptying it of tension and toxins with your exhalation. Let the breath cleanse you of your tension as a river cleanses its bed.

When you have visited every part of your body with your breath, fill your entire body at once with light and energy, and empty it of tension and toxins. Finally, imagine your breath filling up the space beyond your skin with light and energy. Each time you breathe in, fill your lungs, your body, and the space around your body. Create a bubble or an envelope of energy around your body with your breath. Focus on the sensory information coming from all parts of your body, especially the skin and the energy envelope. When you are ready, open your eyes.

Energy Qualities

Endow your energy with a quality. Imagine that your energy is water; see how it affects your movement. Give your energy weight; breathe into the floor through the soles of your feet. Focus all of your energy into the floor below like roots, and see how you feel, listen to the impulses that percolate up, move the way your energy dictates. Endow your energy with a color and let it inform your movement. Let your energy beam in all directions like the sun, let it be a black hole, let it stream up into the sky, let it be a steel wedge, let it become a dinosaur's tail. Thus you can inform character, inspire choreography, infuse the atmosphere.

Energy Mirror

By creating a physical connection among performers, energy work builds an ensemble.

In pairs, face each other at arm's length. Breathe into the space between your bodies, charge the space, establish an energy connection. Do a leaderless mirror, focusing on the energy between you, allowing the energy to connect your movements. Endow the connection with a quality—like rubber bands, springs, or magnets—and let the energy move you; play with it.

8. Rhythmic Exercises

Rhythmic exercises sharpen performers' awareness of how they interrelate as sculptors of space and time.

Bob Francesconi teaches acting and movement at the North Carolina School of the Arts in Winston-Salem. He uses what he calls rhythmic exercises: abstract group exercises about recognizing and responding to movement impulses. Rhythmic exercises translate elements of jazz improvisation, with its textures, rhythms, dynamics, and consecutive soloists, into movement.

In a beginning rhythmic exercise, one person leads. She initiates a repetitive, rhythmic movement, aware of shaping space and time. She can execute a simple hand clap or a complex leap. She repeats the movement until a strong impulse to change hits her. The other players respond with rhythmic movements that relate to hers. They may choose contrapuntal or complementary movement; they may echo, enlarge, or shrink her movement; they may oppose, twist, locomote, or mock it—as long as they respond directly to the leader's impulse.

If the leader begins by squatting and beating the floor with her hands, responses might be to do the same; to jump in time with or opposed to the rhythm; to run in a pattern in time with or opposed to the rhythm; to remain still or sweep back and forth across the floor, using eight of the beats on the floor for one sweep. When the leader feels from the group a strong impulse to change, she begins a different repetitive motion, and the group responds.

The players focus on the group and the initiator. They respond quickly and directly to the initiator's movement with simple, strong choices. They cultivate an awareness of the frame of the space and their relationship to and within it. Each mover stays connected to the whole.

First Variation: When the leader initiates a change, others may choose either to respond or not to respond by continuing with their previous movement.

Second Variation: The leader initiates a change and the others respond, choose not to respond, or make a bold choice. The bold choice springs from a deep connection to the group, a gut-level response that forces the bold choice. It may or may not relate to the leader. It may move the group to a new place. The guidelines are: don't deny what is going on in the space; feel the group energy in your gut (don't just look for it) and go with it; support the action. If someone makes a bold choice and the others in the group respond to it, then the bold chooser becomes the new leader. The old leader becomes a member of the group. Rhythmic exercises teach leading and following skills.

9. Moving

Judith DeWitt, a dancer and choreographer based in Chattanooga, Tennessee, said,

> I have gotten ideas for pieces from going into the studio by myself, being with myself, and just moving, and finding out what is going on emotionally and physically. . . . Often I put on music in those sessions to, at least, have some other presence, or a mood, to keep me from getting stuck in certain mind-talk. . . .
>
> For my first solo piece . . . I went into the studio and I found some music I didn't know, written for the victims of Hiroshima. I began some stretching and breathing with the music on, which eventually developed into an improvisation about being a plant or a tree that was growing. As that improvisation expanded over a period of months, it evolved into something personal and complex, which demanded more structure. I brought in Leslie Morris, artistic director of The Dance Unit, the company to which I belonged at the time, to collaborate with me. Her ability to ask the right questions and her willingness to work with my answers enabled me to retain my original images and movement qualities while finding ways to connect and move them through space, giving the dance a definite physical and emotional shape. But the dance originated with music and breath and movement, without any preconceived ideas, other than just to be there.

10. Bringing an Object to Play With

Dumpsters and thrift stores can spark new ideas.

In TOUCH we rehearsed one year in a vacant supermarket. For an idea I was developing, I brought in some dolls. One day I arrived to see company member Skip Mendler riding his bicycle around the space, using a broom as a polo mallet and a doll as a ball. He hit the doll with the broom, rode to it, swung the broom over his head, and hit it again. When my colleague Jef arrived, he grabbed a doll and pitched it to Skip, who swung his broom at it like a baseball bat. Skip dismounted, and they played baseball, reciting a play-by-play punctuated by the sound of a broom thwacking a doll. From that game we hatched a performance about the relationship between personal and global violence.

Once, we cut a hole in the bottom of an empty TV console and took turns wearing it on our heads. We eventually lit it up inside and used it in a piece. Another time I brought in a stack of form-feed computer paper from a dumpster. We played with the paper—ripping it, crumpling it, dressing in it, tossing it—until we were wading in a sea of paper. A piece grew from that session.

Sue Schroeder, artistic director of CORE Performance Company in Atlanta, talked about beginning a piece by improvising with personal objects:

> Our first improvisations were just a day: bring some meaningful item to the rehearsal. And do their first rehearsal based on the meaningful item, or on some relationship to the meaningful item. . . . It was mainly to get them to connect and to begin their investment to the piece from a very personal place. . . . We did that for many days: combined them, ordered them differently. . . .

Eric Beatty, formerly of Touchstone Theatre in Bethlehem, Pennsylvania, said that to research their show *Don't Drop Grandma,* the company didn't start with a theme. For two weeks they each brought in whatever "got them hot":

> I brought in certain paintings, and I said, "Imagine you are this character, and write or speak something from that character's point of view." I looked at the Hopper painting of the diner, *Nighthawks,* and I picked out six or seven elements, like shadow and café and overcoat and hat, and I gave that list to everybody, and I had them write a piece using all of those elements. So everybody performed their piece after a half-hour or forty-five minutes. . . . I didn't show them the picture. So they came up with four very different, interesting ten-minute skits.

11. Making Something
Andrew Long, a choreographer in the Austin-based troupe Johnson/Long Dance Company, said that he often starts a dance piece by making a painting. The painting informs him about architecture, mood, and theme.

Jyl Hewston, who cofounded Theatre Plexus near Washington, D.C., in the 1970s and worked with Howling Woolf Theatre in Northern California in the early 1990s, said that the performers in Plexus made some masks, then asked: "What can we do with these masks?"

It was harder for us to do what you're supposed to do, you know: "What do we want to say, and what is the best form to say it with?" The easier way is to ask, "What do we do with these masks?" We didn't start with, "What's the point? Why are we doing this?"

Make something, and while you make it stay open to ideas and fantasies and write them down. When you finish your project, look at what you've made. Pay attention to feelings, urges, images, sounds, or memories that bubble up. Touch it. Do a round with it.

12. Going Somewhere

Lin Hixson, artistic director of Goat Island performance group in Chicago, said that the group traveled to Ireland for the Croagh Patrick pilgrimage:

> It was a very rigorous climb, and there were 30,000 people on the pilgrimage. . . . We each had a very specific system of approach. I did spatial diagrams of anything of interest to me. Matthew [Goulish] was appropriating text each day from different things that he observed. Karen [Christopher] was taping thirty seconds of sound each day. Tim [McCain] was . . . making movement from observed things and making dances. . . .

You don't have to cross an ocean. Take a research trip to your local police department, bakery, hospital, mall, or homeless shelter.

13. Practicing Skills

Robert Alexander founded and directed Living Stage Theatre Company in Washington, D.C., which runs workshops and creates interactive performances for young people about vital issues in their lives. He described their workshops as a way of turning people on to their creativity,

> allowing them to experience their imagination, to fall in love with their imagination, to revere their imagination, and to know how essential their imagination is. It is the most important organ in their body, and to quote Albert Einstein, "Imagination is more important than knowledge." So that they can . . . live their daily life as an artist.
>   I have a prescription for life that I give people, which is the creation of three poems a day and three stories a day improvisa-

tionally, saying it out loud, and in nine months they'll be a fantastic improvisational poet and a fantastic improvisational storyteller, which is our birthright. I believe that Mother Nature created the human being to think and learn and create as our natural biological function, and when you deny people that, you drive them crazy. . . .

Jyl Hewston said that in Theatre Plexus they invented material based on what they could do. "We can play these instruments; we can juggle; what kind of story can we concoct with music and juggling?"

Daily practice of skills serves as a renewable resource. While you practice, stay awake to thoughts or fantasies; follow them. Ask, "What is the story here? Where can this go? What if I do it this way? What does this remind me of? How does this feel? Who could I be? Where? What does this mean? What do I want?"

14. Round-Table Discussions
In the early 1980s, Bond Street Theatre Coalition sat around a table and discussed burning issues of the day. Through discussion, they settled on a theme for a show, which they named *Powerplay*, about how the military-industrial complex profits from producing the means for the destruction of the world. Next, some of them researched the military-industrial complex, while others researched mythology for ways to dramatize the story.

15. Storytelling
Stories overflow with creative juices for performers. We grow up hearing stories—fairy tales, folktales, religious stories, family stories. Have everyone tell the same story, one after another; or have several people tell the story together. Unravel the essential plot. Tell the story silently. Sing it. Rap it.

Close your eyes and listen, or take notes, or act it out. Notice images, movements, sensations, colors, and sounds the story calls up. Talk about the parts that resonate. Talk about parallel stories from other sources.

16. The Little Black Book
Shelley Wallace, of Jest in Time Theatre in Halifax, Nova Scotia, revealed that company members carry "a little black book" and write ideas as they occur. Five Lesbian Brothers keep a log when they tour,

because they generate spontaneous hilarity on the road, which they later explore in rehearsal. The comedian Steve Allen carried a micro-cassette recorder in his pocket. He recorded half-baked ideas, categorizing each one—this goes in the book; this goes in political jokes.

Keep a journal—on paper, videotape, audiotape, or computer. Make entries daily. Don't censor; just record. Trust that some useful material will surface. When you review what you have, pull out whatever piques your interest and play with it in rehearsal.

17. Free-Writing

When Five Lesbian Brothers went on a writing retreat, they awoke at the same time each morning, sat silently at the kitchen table, and free-wrote for fifteen minutes. They read to each other whatever they wanted to share.

Free-writing generally means you write for a predetermined amount of time; you write whatever occurs to you; once you start, you do not stop; if you run dry, you write nonsense, or rhymes, or you repeat; you don't bother with grammar, punctuation, or spelling, and you do not censor or correct. If you use a big piece of paper, you can write words and make shapes at the same time; for example, several ideas can spoke from a central hub, or one sentence can bridge two related ideas.[9]

A good time to free-write is when you wake up, when your subconscious mind is closest to consciousness. If you fill up two or three pages, or write for twenty minutes daily, you will generate some drivel, but you will also produce some precious creative gems.

18. Someone Else's Writing

Shakespeare borrowed from classical and contemporary literature. So can we!

Cornerstone Theater Company of Santa Monica, California adapts classical plays to fit individual communities. For a Mississippi residency they translated *Romeo and Juliet* into a Southern vernacular and cast the Montagues and Capulets as Blacks and Whites. They go to a town, listen to how people speak and what issues concern them, set up their computer with the original play on disk, and rewrite the play to fit the local scene.

According to Bill Allard of Duck's Breath Mystery Theater, Dan Coffey used to read the newspaper aloud:

"Here's a piece about a woman who locked up all her books with her dog," he'd say. And somebody would say, "Well, that's interesting." And somebody else would say, "Yeah, the dog-woman." And the piece wouldn't necessarily end up being about a dog or a woman or books or anything originally in the idea. You've got to start somewhere.

Hilarie Burke-Porter founded Silent Partners in Asheville, North Carolina. She and her partner, Connie Schrader, read about Transactional Analysis, and created a performance based on T.A.'s theory of the different parts of the self. Porter got an idea for another piece from a matchbook she picked up in a bar. Jef, cofounder of TOUCH, got an idea from a Dutch comic book in a friend's bathroom.

19. TV, Movies, and Radio
Bob Paton, who worked with the Living Theatre in the 1990s and previously with Playback Theatre, saw a TV interview with Joseph Campbell, in which Campbell said, "Dreams are like myths, and myths are like dreams." Campbell's statement hooked Paton. His fascination with mythology and dreams led him to found Theatre of Dreams.

20. Dreams
Keep paper and pen next to your bed. Cultivate the habit of writing down your dreams when you wake up.

Bob Paton's Manhattan-based Theatre of Dreams asks audience members to tell their dreams for the company to enact. At the end of each performance, the audience collaborates to invent a modern myth based on those dreams that the performers re-create. Paton said,

> There's much evidence that most tribal societies were much into dreams. They told each other their dreams; it was a part of the ritual of their daily lives, to meet as families, around a circle, when they got up in the morning and share their dreams. . . . They thought that dreams could portend the future; they felt that dreams had a healing effect. . . . The myths that we have from earlier peoples probably had their origins in dreams. It's logical to assume that, because they're so much alike. It's the same language and the same structure and the same themes.

21. Meditation

Meditation opens a door to our creativity.

Laura Bertin, a performer from Wayne, Pennsylvania, likes to start rehearsals with ten minutes of silent meditation. Sometimes she lights a candle and focuses on it.

You can buy books and tapes that have guided meditations. There are many ways to meditate: moving meditations, like walking meditation, tai chi, or yoga; or stationary meditations, like lying down or sitting za-zen or meditating on a painting. Here is one example of a sitting meditation.[10]

Sit in a chair with your feet flat on the floor, your hands resting on your thighs, and your spine erect. Close your eyes. Take a deep breath and feel where it goes into your body. As you exhale, feel the breath passing through your throat and leaving through your mouth. Count, "One."

Count each breath, from one to ten, and from one to ten, again, for five minutes or longer. When ideas and images arise, let them go and return your focus to your breath. If you feel your muscles relaxing or your body getting lighter, fine. Don't judge or praise yourself.

It sounds easy to quiet the mind and focus on the breath, but it requires concentration. Our minds have the seductive agility of television; meditation turns off the TV. Our minds don't want to turn off. Meditation strengthens concentration skills.

Many of the performers I interviewed meditate. Images, ideas, and sensations surface as you meditate. After meditating, move and vocalize however your internal impulses dictate.[11]

Hub Meditation

Dancer and choreographer Daniel Nagrin describes a hub meditation in *Dance and the Specific Image*. Close your eyes. Empty your head with your breath. When you are ready, a watcher says a sentence with this structure: "Someone or something is doing something." Like, "Someone or something is rising and falling." Or, "Someone or something is searching for someone or something." They do not name the subject of the sentence; they do name the action. When you hear the sentence about searching, for example, one after another, let various images of various creatures searching for various things come into the hub of your mind. The image that keeps recurring is the one to follow for further exploration.

Given enough time in a focused meditation, the mind will find it-self occupied with an image that dominates all others. . . . It mat-ters not whether the image is attractive or repulsive, whether the image is fascinating or on its surface quite dull, that is the image to work on. . . .

The last thing one should do is to hunt for a "good image," a "creative image," an "exciting image." . . . The basic dictum to the work says: if it isn't personal, it isn't worth working on and it has nothing to do with art.[12]

22. A Strong Emotional Life Experience

Tom Keegan, of the gay interdisciplinary performing duo from Los Angeles, Keegan and Lloyd, said, "A strong emotional life experience seems to carry a wholeness about it that has a beginning, middle, and end, and everything else. The piece is already made in life. We just have to discover it."

Bring the experience into rehearsal. Compose a rap about it. Construct a still life of it.

OK, I'm Trying One of These Suggestions, Now What?

Now that you have tried some of the twenty-two ways to get an idea for a piece, and you've found an idea that has piqued your curiosity, try any of the other twenty-two ways to move your idea forward. Once you pick, for example, a strong emotional experience from your life as your idea, you can tell stories about it, free-write about it, make an object, improvise, do rounds, research it, and have round-table discussions on it.

For each trial, have someone watch, tape, or take notes. After each trial, talk about

- what you liked
- what it reminded you of; what it could lead to; the unrelated idea it gave you
- what you felt: the kinetic kick, the poignant episode, the arresting moment
- what parts were visually interesting; where you found a telling juxtaposition

- what story, conflict, or relationship you see
- what interesting twist you'd like to give it
- what part was funny
- what title would add a new dimension.

Look for anything that works and write it down. At this stage, do not judge your work. A new idea lives a precarious life. It needs nourishment and warmth. Imagine criticizing a baby who is learning to walk: "No! that's too wide a stance. No! You're leaning too far back. Stop swaying back and forth!" Your criticism would paralyze the poor baby.

Likewise for a new idea. Talk about its possibilities. ("Look at that grin. She's going to be president!") Do not mention its drawbacks. Do not allow your fellow players to paralyze it with negative talk. Have faith that your exploration of it will lead to a worthwhile work.

Graduation

In this chapter I've assumed that you didn't have a starting idea. Once you try a few of the suggested ways to get an idea, something will catch your fancy. Latch onto it. It doesn't have to be brilliant; it can be banal—a trick, a toy, a photograph. Now you have an idea. Eureka!

Jump in and play with it—write a poem, build a model, collect metaphors. Now you are collecting material.

Trust your impulses. The creative process has no set order. You walk through it one step at a time, but not in a straight line; you meander, or you hop from stone to stone. Each step informs you about what and where the next step might be.

Notes

1. Daniel Goleman, *Emotional Intelligence* (New York: Bantam Books, 1995), p. 85.

2. For more on rounds, see Tony Montanaro with Karen Hurll Montanaro, *Mime Spoken Here: The Performer's Portable Workshop* (Gardiner, ME: Tilbury House, 1995), pp. 146–154.

3. Steven A. Beebe and John T. Masterson, *Communicating in Small Groups: Principles and Practices* (Glenview, IL: HarperCollins, 1989), pp. 184–186; Charles Pavitt, "What (Little) We Know About Formal Group Discussion Procedures," in *Small Group Research* (London) 24, no. 2 (1993): 227–228.

4. Tony Montanaro with Karen Hurll Montanaro, *Mime Spoken Here,* p. 161.

5. Ibid., pp. 154–158.

6. Viola Spolin, *Improvisation for the Theater, A Handbook of Teaching and Directing Techniques* (Evanston, IL: Northwestern University Press, 1985); Keith Johnstone, *Impro! Improvisation and the Theatre,* with an introduction by Irving Wardle (London and Boston: Faber and Faber, 1979); Daniel Nagrin, *Dance and the Specific Image: Improvisation* (Pittsburgh, PA: University of Pittsburgh Press, 1994); Tony Montanaro with Karen Hurll Montanaro, *Mime Spoken Here,* pp. 146–154; Lynda Belt and Rebecca Stockley, *Improvisation Through TheatreSports: A Curriculum to Improve Acting Skills* (Seattle, WA: Thespis Productions, 1991).

7. Susan Ribner and Dr. Richard Chin, *The Martial Arts* (New York: Harper and Row, 1984), p. 27.

8. To learn more about energy, go to holistic health centers, New Age massage therapists, and schools of yoga, karate, or tai chi.

9. For more about free-writing and the creative process, see Natalie Goldberg's *Writing Down the Bones: Freeing the Writer Within* (Boston and London: Shambhala, 1986); and Julia Cameron's *The Artist's Way: A Spiritual Path to Higher Creativity* (New York: G. P. Putnam's Sons, 1992.)

10. Jessica MacBeth, *Moon over Water: The Path of Meditation* (Bath, England: Gateway Books, 1990), p. 34.

11. For a catalog of meditation tapes, write: Gateway Books, The Hollies, Wellow, Bath BA28QJ, England, or, The Great Tradition, 11270 Clayton Creek Road, Lower Lake, CA 95457.

12. Daniel Nagrin, *Dance and the Specific Image,* pp. 55–57.

2 The Next Step

How to Generate Material About Your Idea and How to Begin to Shape It

This chapter provides a loose format for moving your work forward and suggests questions to ask to find the next step, research tools for gathering material, and ways to give a preliminary shape to the material you gather.

Now that you have latched onto an idea, you need to generate material about it. Material is anything that contributes to your knowledge of the piece: phrases, metaphors, movement phrases, gestures, improvs, notes, objects, character sketches, moments of action, conflicts, pictures, diagrams, music. At the beginning of the process, simply gather material. It won't all end up in the final product and it won't all be brilliant. You will cull the germane parts later. At this early stage, keep open to all possibilities.

Start a file for your idea and put each discovery you make into it. Draw characters, costumes, masks, environments. Diagram build, structure, and design. Write about the themes, philosophical underpinning, symbology, background. Invent biographies for your characters. Describe the mood, color, atmosphere, and world of the piece. Write metaphors, dreams, memories.

When you get into the studio, choose one aspect of your idea that you know something about, and devise a game or exercise to help you discover more about it. Do something—anything—with it. Use the exercises in Chapter One, in this chapter, in the next two chapters, and make up your own.

Liz Lerman, artistic director of the Dance Exchange, a multigenerational company in Takoma Park, Maryland, says

> The actual discovery of particular improvisational structures which we would use to go figure things out, that alters completely from piece to piece, from moment to moment. And in fact, that's probably one of the most creative things I do, is to say, OK, here's the thing we're trying to figure out now, what's an improvisational structure that can help us discover that? The subject itself can suggest the structure.

A Format for Moving Your Work Forward

1. Look at what you have.
2. Choose one element to work on.
3. Articulate what you want to try.
4. Give everyone one job related to the element.
5. Try it.
6. Look at what you tried.
7. Discuss what works.
8. Decide what to keep; write it down.
9. Choose a new element to work on.
10. Articulate clearly what you want to try.
11. Give everyone one job.
12. Try it.
13. Look at what you tried. . . .

It's simple: work on one thing at a time, continue to improvise, and keep what works. Be prepared for surprises; some of the best ideas tap you on the back while you are looking elsewhere.

Asking Questions to Find the Next Step

Ask many questions. Good questions drive creative thought. Here are some questions to help you along your creative journey. Some of them may bridge the transition from what you just did to what you might do next. I am indebted to C. W. Metcalf, performer and corporate trainer, for most of them.

What did we just do? What were the problems? What do we want to keep? Where does this get us? How does what we just did relate to what we already have? What is the next step? What do we need to decide? Given what we have, where does the piece want to go? Given the character(s), what choices are available now? What actions are logical? What does the scene need? What are we trying to say? How do we solve this problem? How do we move the action forward?

Why are we doing this piece? Is it news? Who needs to see it? Who is interested?

What is original about it? What do people know about its subject matter? What clichés, metaphors, and images pertain to it? How can we capitalize on them? How do we challenge them?

What are the underlying assumptions? Are these assumptions true for us? for our audience? What logic do these assumptions set up? Is the piece true to that logic? Where does the piece break the logic? Is that OK?

Who is our audience? How do we connect our piece to them? Why do these people need to see this piece? How do we want to affect them? How will they be changed by it?

What is the piece about? What does the piece imply? What is the main theme? What is the point?

What is the statement? How can we best make the statement? What media most eloquently express the statement? What are the most compelling visual and aural ways to make the statement?

How do we communicate the world to the audience? Do they get it?

Is it a comedy? Does it have a happy ending? Is it a tragedy?

What is the nature of the conflict? How do we resolve it?

What symbols are, or should be, in the piece? What do they symbolize? What does the audience understand about the symbology?

Where is the piece taking place? Is that the best place for it to be, in terms of statement, logic, possibilities? Does the audience recognize the place?

Who is each character? How do we reveal the relationships between characters? What do the characters want and need? Do they get what they want and need? How? Why don't they? What obstacles must they overcome? What do they want and need, moment to moment? Where did they come from before the piece began? Where will they go when it ends?

What are the essential moments without which the piece won't make sense? What do they say? How do they move the piece forward? Do we highlight or weight them adequately?

What are the human qualities in the piece?

What is the emotional resolution of the piece?

Research Tools for Gathering Material

It doesn't matter *which* structure you use to gather material, but it does matter that you pick a structure.

How do groups generate material collaboratively? Most groups use brainstorming; otherwise, each group travels its own road. They embrace a variety of research tools, from history lectures to storytelling to imagining to banging off the walls. In addition to the exercises in Chapters One, Three, and Four, you can use any of the following research and gathering tools.

Lectures: What Historical Events Relate to the Theme?
The San Francisco Mime Troupe's founder, R. G. Davis, described how they developed *The Life and Times of Che Guevara* in the 1960s.[1] Company members met regularly for a Latin American history class. Each member researched a topic, and lectured the company. Outside experts also lectured.

According to Dan Chumley, current director of the Troupe, when the company begins a new work, they first talk about whom they want to reach and what message they want to convey—those questions undergird their writing process—then they do individual research, which they share with the group.

Story Theater: What Is the Story?
Much material can come in the form of stories. A simple transition from lecture information to rehearsal activity is Story Theater, a form developed by Paul Sills in Chicago. As one person narrates events from lecture research, others perform the actions described. The actors thus physically embody the information, allowing observers to see dramatic and choreographic potential.

Interviews: What Are the Major Themes?

The Dakota Theatre Caravan toured the western states with original plays about the people and history of South Dakota. For their first play, company members interviewed South Dakotans and convened daily to discuss their interviews. Then they narrowed the focus of topics for the next day's interviews.

D. Scott Glasser, one of the original Caravan members, explained:

> We gathered in Yankton. . . . We set some guidelines for ourselves about interviews, and canvassed the town. We'd go into bars and stop people on the streets. . . . We called everyone we knew.
>
> We quickly put together some music so that we could sing for our supper. They would give us supper; we would entertain them . . . and then we would split up and interview them about their lives—"What matters to you?" "What's foremost on your mind?" "Define South Dakota"—real big topics. Then we would gather that information, discuss it, refocus what we wanted to ask, and then go back out again.

What Structure Might Illustrate the Major Themes?

Primary topics came to the forefront very quickly. . . . Then we had a round-table discussion to structure it. We would sit down and quickly structure a play. First we would talk about the major themes. What is it we are going to write about? And we would have a session of throwing any of the ideas that we could together: about what form the play could take, or what type of characters it might be about. Each time it was a matter of focusing it, clarifying it.

We would do an outline. . . . When we agreed what the major themes were, we outlined a structure with those themes and detailed it. We broke the theme down into subthemes. It was a matter of delving deeper into it and seeing what we could come up with. . . . It's an improvisation, essentially, a group improv.

We also split up our responsibilities. Some of us would write while others did research. If we felt we really needed personal stories on this issue, some of the group would do another round of interviews about specific topics, say, World War II in South Dakota, or the Depression. . . .

We always had music. One of our company was composing and writing songs. Others wrote lyrics. . . .

Doug [Paterson, founder of the Caravan] would bring the script together under one voice, essentially. He'd gather all the parts of the script together into a final draft.

Recording Interviews

If you use interviews, get a portable tape recorder with a counter and an omnidirectional microphone, and lots of cheap tapes. Take notes during the interviews: outline the topics discussed and jot down the counter numbers so you can locate the juicy bits later.

Have a lawyer draw up a consent form, and make copies. Ask everybody you interview to sign the consent form. Get a broadly worded release allowing you to record, quote, paraphrase, print, publish, and broadcast in all media. Then you can use the source material in performance and promotions. In addition to the consent form, get taped permissions at the beginning of each interview from each interviewee, allowing you to record and use the recording.

Clichés and Metaphors

Mat Schwarzman, codirector of the Institute for Urban Arts in Oakland, California, asks the youth he works with to cull the metaphors and clichés that emerge from interviews, and then to create graphics or characters from them. When interviews about welfare policy referred to "welfare queens," performers developed a character sketch from the stereotype. Clichés like "deadbeat dads," "a thousand points of light," "war on poverty," and "safety net" could lend themselves to images, characters, or sketches.

Town Meetings: What Do People Know About the Topic?

When the Road Company in Johnson City, Tennessee, began writing their play, *Horsepower*, they held town meetings and invited the public to talk about the Tennessee Valley Authority's electrification of eastern Tennessee and the proposed nuclear power plant. They asked how electricity changed people's lives. They also did historical research on the T.V.A.

If you hold town meetings, frame questions that go to the heart of your subject. Facilitate the meetings so all can speak, and record them. Ask participants to sign a release form permitting you to use the conversation.

Essential Sketches: What Are the Essential Elements?

After gathering stories through interviews or town meetings, one way to proceed is to list all the compelling stuff—characters, stories, places, conflicts, images—that stick out in your imagination. Then split up and make brief sketches describing the essence of each one. Show them to each other and discuss them.

Research What We Don't Know About the Topic?

Pennsylvania's Bloomsburg Theatre Ensemble put together a play from letters to the editors of newspapers. Actor/director Gerard Stropnicky sketched the process.

> There was a big research component. . . . We met with the editor of the local paper. . . . In four weeks, we spent about half the time in the library. Everybody got a roll of dimes [to make copies of the interesting letters].
>
> I set up the parameters . . . for example, we were going to stick just to letters . . . to local newspapers. . . . We established certain themes: wacko letters, letters that start with "The President of the U.S. is . . ." letters about dogs. . . . Everybody had a list of topics and a roll of dimes, and a microfilm machine, and took different decades of different newspapers, and literally rolled through the newspapers. . . .

Character Sketches: What Characters Belong?

> Then they would bring back a pile of letters that they had found. . . . Then we would take an hour to read them to each other. And then I would send them off to work on their own, to develop them into beginning character pieces—duets, trios. . . . Then they would come back and do them for each other.

Site Walks: What Stories Do People Tell About the Place?

Jeff Mather is an Atlanta artist who builds site sculptures in collaboration with the communities that hire him. He often works with schools. He includes students, teachers, administrators, parents, and custodians on his design team. He said,

> I do a site walk: to take my design team out and walk the landscape and stop and talk and collect stories . . . stories about place, specifically about place. We will walk through the landscape, and they will say, "Well, you know, we're not supposed to go back behind the trees in this part of the playground. We love to when the teacher's not looking." There are stories about what happens in the gully behind the trees. Or in the courtyard, one year a Native American cultural visitor set up an enormous teepee, and for-

evermore, the kids go, "This is where the teepee was." It's a sacred spot, they will always remember it. They still see it in there, even though it's gone. So there are all these layers of stories and history of the place that I want to hear before we ever sit down and draw and design.

Mather photographs the site and makes faint photocopies of the photos, which he hands out to the community designers. Each person draws his idea for a sculpture on the photo. If he has access to computers, Mather scans his photos of the site into the computers, and the community designers sketch their designs directly onto the screen image of the site.

Personal Stories: What Is My Personal Connection to the Work?

Martha Boesing, one of the founders and director of At the Foot of the Mountain Theatre, a feminist collective in Minneapolis, spoke about finding a personal connection to the work. In describing a play they wrote about rape, she said,

> Every play that we entered into, we started with the question, what does this mean in my own life? How have I prostituted myself? How have I raped, or been raped? Even if you hadn't been raped by a stranger in an alley with a knife, or even if you hadn't been physically raped, but maybe you've been mentally raped. . . . We each kept, every day, telling our stories, telling our personal stories, every day, telling our personal stories.

What Is the Point of View?

When you find a story that intrigues you, have each person tell the same story from a different point of view. Tell it through movement. Tell it in song.

Story Pulling: What Do We Remember About It?

Los Angeles–based director Steven Kent founded and directed the Company Theatre in the 1960s and directed the Provisional Theatre in the 1970s. He sometimes worked with TOUCH as guest director and dramaturg.

One piece he helped us with was about a lesbian's coming-out process. Before we started work, Kent spent a week "story pulling" with the company member whose life formed the basis of the piece. He taped their conversation as he asked her open-ended questions, such as "What do you remember of your mother?" "What was that like?" "And then?" As she spoke, he outlined—with Post-it Notes on newsprint—themes, story threads, characters, and scenes.

Mission Statement: What Are Our Goals?

When we came together to create the piece, we started with a transcript of the taped conversation, Kent's outline, and a rough sketch of a short script the company member had written. First we collaborated to craft a mission statement that answered these questions: What are we doing? What is the point of doing it? Who is it for? Why are we doing it? How do we want to affect the audience?

We talked about our personal identification with the work and reviewed the transcript together, looking for what could fit into the piece and how. Then we started adjusting Kent's outline and roughing out the script.

Image Exercise: What Images Pertain to the Theme?

Imagery is a rich source of material. Tony Montanaro uses image exercises to research movement and movement qualities.[2] You can do an image exercise on anything that moves: animals, characters, machines.

To begin, stand, sit, or lie comfortably. Close your eyes. Clear your mind. Breathe and relax. When ready, allow the image of the creature you are studying, say, a chimpanzee, to appear in your mind. Watch how he moves on the movie screen of your mind. You can ask him to move in a particular way—eat, walk, groom, climb. You can zoom in to examine a specific part—the hands, or face.

Ask the chimpanzee to stand if you are standing, sit if you are sitting, or to lie down. Stand, sit, or lie as he does. Keeping his image alive in your mind, follow what he does as he does it. Initiate nothing. Move only when and how he does. Keeping the image in your mind, open your eyes and continue to follow whatever he does. Look for details, like what his fur looks like, and let them infuse your movement. When you have fully embodied the chimp, gradually transform into a human with chimpanzee qualities.

Even beginners discover a strong connection and accurate, unself conscious movement with image exercises. Take turns working and watching others work.

Circles Exercise: What Is the Main Action?

Daniel Nagrin founded the Workgroup, a New York dance improv company of the early 1970s. His circles exercise provides another pathway to research images and explore movement.[3]

Start by emptying the mind, relaxing, and being present. When you are ready, signal your observer. She says a sentence with this structure: "Someone (or something) is doing something." It could be, "A child is reaching"; "A woman is running"; "An ocean is rising and falling;" "A cheetah is stalking."

Let the sentence penetrate your mind as a picture. Get specific about who is doing what and how. How old is the child? Boy or girl? What color is her hair, her eyes, her skin, her clothing? Where is she? What is she reaching for? Why?

When you have gotten as specific as you can, start with your scalp and hair, and imagine your scalp and hair becoming the scalp and hair of that creature doing that activity. When you feel you have transformed your scalp and hair, move to your face and neck. Let your face and neck become that child's face and neck reaching. Take all the time you need, and move down your body, concentrating on one area at a time, exploring the image with each area fully, then moving on. When you have covered every area, put it all together. Aim for complete physical commitment to the image.

Banging off the Walls:
What Fairy Tales Connect to the Work?

Gay performing artists Tom Keegan and Davidson Lloyd comprise Keegan and Lloyd of Los Angeles. Keegan said, when they begin working on a new idea,

> We start to improvise: just sort of bang off the walls. For *Naked and in Love*, we invented a fairy tale for it. One of us started the story, the other picked it up, and we wove in, using elements from traditional fairy tale structure. Then we repeat, and repeat. Then we discuss it. "Let's have this element or that element."

It's important to begin [by] standing up, talking, and moving: shaping things through the body. That way we know it inside; there's the immediacy of being in the moment. It comes from a very deep place.

Lloyd added,

Moving around shifts things. Just standing still, your brain gets stuck in one place. If you're moving, pulling yourself through space . . . images happen that may not happen if you're just sitting. We repeat and repeat and repeat and repeat. In the process, images start to appear. They keep coming back. After a while, you start to say, "Oh. That's an image that obviously wants to be in this piece."

Keegan said,

We bang around and bang around, and then record it and start writing things down and shaping it. We write some monologues independently. We go over each other's material, and edit. We make suggestions and fight over what we want to keep.

What Songs Belong to the Theme and Characters?

Lloyd uses an exercise he learned from Medicine Show Theatre Ensemble in New York. They choose a song for each character and run through sections singing the song. They will try a scene as an opera. Once they went through a murder scene singing "He's got the Whole World in His Hands." The incongruity allows other things to happen, and can distill a part to its essence.

Trying Anything: How Can We Break Our Preconceptions?

In his book *Group Theatre,* Brian Clark remarked how difficult it is to get beyond clichés when improvising scenes for a new piece. To get over the cliché hump, he recommends breaking all links with your previous ideas—try anything.

- Do it blindfolded.
- Allow each character to speak only one word or gibberish or to chant.
- Do it walking backward, or as monkeys or centipedes.
- Introduce new elements and environments: a beach, a tower, a fair, a coal mine.

- Have the men play women and the women play men.
- Act it with only one part of the body.[4]

Mindful Chaos: What Is Funny About It?

Bill Allard gave me an impromptu replay of what might happen in the studio during a Duck's Breath rehearsal.

> Here's how it goes in rehearsal, five guys talking and trying all at once.
>   "I've got an idea about the box."
>   "OK, here's the box."
>   "What size is it?"
>   "How about this big?"
>   "OK."
>   "How about this size?"
>   "OK."
>   "It's blue, it's a blue box."
>   "That's hilarious."
>   "So what if I put it on my head like this?"
>   "OK."
>   "Or get inside it?"
>   "OK."
>   "Now, we'll stand behind him and say, 'Box, box, box, more than a box.'"
>   "No, that's too boring."
>   "How about faster and faster?"
>   "Yeah, great!"

Allard recalled a lesson they learned early on.

> We wrote a whole show in four hours. Everybody was holding their crotches, jumping up and down laughing. The next day we came in, and we couldn't remember what we had done. When you're working, somebody says an idea, and you add to it and add to it. . . . Somebody has got to write it down.

Duck's Breath's basic process goes like this:

1. Sit and talk about it.
2. Write it down.
3. Stand up and make it funny.

Giving Shape to Your Material

What Do We Want to Say? What Media Will Say It Most Powerfully?

By now you have gathered a mass of material about your idea by writing, discussing, inventing exercises, using exercises from this book, and improvising. If you haven't done so already, it's time to choose an organizing principle so you can shape the work. Sometimes its shape comes with the initial idea. Sometimes walking or talking through the parts you like will suggest a shape. And sometimes you produce a pile of material, and you have no idea how to mold it into a coherent whole.

At this point in the process, I often feel as if I am wrestling a protean monster. I try to fit all the material into one form, but I get ugly bulges, gaping holes, and inconsistencies. I ask myself two questions: What framework works best for my intentions? Which parts belong?

There are many approaches to this phase. In order to create a harmonious whole out of your pile, you need to make choices about genre (comedy, drama, farce); sequence of events (beginning, middle, and end); structure (number of scenes, through lines, climax, denouement); and characterization (words and actions must be logical in terms of who the characters are).

What Structure Can the Material Take?

Chapel Hill playwright Sarah Froeber has written three different children's plays using one plot structure. In each play the protagonist and his problem are introduced. He tries three different ways to fix the problem, but an obstacle thwarts him at each try. Then the protagonist or other characters shift their beliefs, and the problem gets resolved.[5]

To uncover your structure, highlight the important moments. Define what you must establish for the piece's progress to make sense. Diagram your structure. Perform it so you can see the bones of your work. There are many ways to structure a piece. Here are a few suggestions.

What Scenes Will Tell the Story?

Joan Schirle teaches writing for actor-creators at The Dell'Arte International School in Blue Lake, California. She tells her students

Once you get an idea, break it down into events and scenes, so everybody knows where they're going. Document how each scene moves the piece along, and know what purpose each scene serves in relationship to the whole. Set minideadlines for yourself: you will have X number of scenes by this time next week; you will have dialogue for this scene tomorrow.

Schirle cautions against waiting until the end of rehearsals to decide on an ending. Work on the ending early on, so you know where you are headed.

What Genre Speaks to Our Audience?
The structure of a piece relies to some extent on its genre. Genre refers to the species, style, type, or form. Joanna Sherman, artistic director of New York's Bond Street Theatre Coalition, explained that they choose a genre for each piece. In the early 1980s they used commedia dell'arte as a genre:

> We got this formula down, and it really works! We take a myth or legend or classical story, and using a commedia dell'arte structure—like the characters: you always have young lovers . . . zanni [clowns] . . . a Pantalone-type that represents the authority . . . a Capitano, who's a military figure—and we take these characters and apply them to a modern-day situation that we would like to address. Plus, we always have a complete musical score, which is like American musical theater.

Choosing the genre gave them a treasure chest of information. Knowing the characters, they could improvise scenes right off the bat; the clowns could create schtick; the musicians could write songs. They now use genres from around the world to inform their writing.

Choosing a genre can speed your writing process. If you know you are working on a Balinese masked dance/drama, you have a structure, a spiritual and cultural foundation, music, instruments, costumes, masks, props, setting, a relationship to the audience, and characters.

Societies invent genres that speak to their own culture. Each genre implies a given structure. Here is a short list of genres that derive from societies around the world.

- Aristotelian comedy and tragedy, epic drama, opera, theater of the absurd, melodrama, magical realism
- circus, clowning, commedia dell'arte, situation comedy, stand-up comedy
- dance: ballet, folk, jazz, modern, postmodern, religious, rhythm, talking
- dance/drama: African drumming and dance; American musical comedy, cabaret, vaudeville, revival, medicine show; Indian Kathakali; Indonesian masked dance/drama; Japanese Noh, Kabuki; Mexican carpas
- film: silent, action/adventure, western, romance, comedy, monster, science fiction
- improvisation, movement theater, performance art, mime, multimedia
- puppetry
- radio drama, rap, poetry, poetry slam, preaching
- storytelling, fairy tales, folktales, mythology
- soap opera, talk show, game show, educational TV

Before you use a genre from another culture, research the form extensively, or else you will end up with a shallow mockery of the form. Exercise care if the genre involves spiritual beliefs. The Balinese believe that the spirits of the gods represented by their masks inhabit the masks when performers assume their roles. They offer sacrifices to the gods before performing. If you do not understand and respect the spiritual meaning of what you are doing, don't do it.

What Sequence of Events Makes the Statement?
C. W. Metcalf encouraged TOUCH to pick a framework—a loose temporary sequence of events—try it out by improvising, and then ask questions. Did it achieve the desired effect? Did it make the statement? Does each section move the piece forward? Which choices work? Which parts are essential? Which parts are redundant? Where are the gaps? What feels awkward? Then revise the sequence and try again.

How Should It Start? and End? Divide the temporary sequence of events into its beginning, middle, and end. Then find the beginning, middle, and end of the beginning; the beginning, middle, and end of the middle, and the beginning, middle, and end of the end. Keep reducing the whole into smaller and smaller parts, until you have the beginning, middle, and end of each beat, or phrase.

What Are the Through Lines and How Do They Evolve?

Through lines are characters, themes, motifs, repeated phrases, symbols, and other elements that weave through a piece. Freelance director/dramaturg Steven Kent, once he has a sketchy sequence, will follow each through line one at a time through the piece, checking for consistency. He articulates how each interrelates with others and how the interrelationships grow over time, and he clarifies their meaning.

When Kent worked with us on one piece, we traced the movements of the "home base," a futon-like prop that symbolized a place of safety for the main character. We walked through our temporary sequence of events, figuring out where the home base was, where the main character stood in relation to it, and how her relationship to it developed over time.

What Sequence Will Build to a Climax?

If you have ten sequences, but don't know how to combine them, use dynamic build as a governing principle. Decide on a satisfying dynamic structure, then arrange the parts to fit. Try it out. For example, start with a big bang, then quickly drop to the lowest, softest, slowest dynamic moment, then gradually build to a climax in a series of jumps and plateaus, and end with a swift, quiet denouement.

Most performance pieces in the Eurocentric tradition build to a climax and follow with a denouement (literally, untying a knot), or resolution. Some pieces (Bill T. Jones' dance, "D-Man in the Water," and many improvised comedy sketches) end at the moment of climax.

What Logical Choices Can the Characters Make?

Much drama concerns how characters change with changing circumstances. Chart the progress you want your characters to make, then structure your material so they can go through the progress you have charted.

Change requires much energy and causes much stress; most humans will not change without vigorous propulsion. Delineate the blows that force your characters to change. If you can't find their impulses to change, you have a gap.

How Do the Characters Develop? Make a graph with a time line and a line for each character, with the major actions of each character marked at the appropriate times. The graph gives you a view of the overall development of your characters.

By now you have an idea; you have opened a file on it; you have researched it in a variety of ways; you have amassed a pile of material; and you have decided, at least temporarily, on a structure or organizing principle. Now you are ready to flesh out the work. The next chapter reveals the one-element-at-a-time process for deepening your work. Carry on.

Notes

1. R. G. Davis, *The San Francisco Mime Troupe: The First Ten Years,* with an introduction by Robert Scheer (Palo Alto, CA: Ramparts Press, 1975), p. 117.

2. Tony Montanaro with Karen Hurll Montanaro, *Mime Spoken Here: The Performer's Portable Workshop* (Gardiner, ME: Tilbury House, 1995), pp. 110–115.

3. Daniel Nagrin, *Dance and the Specific Image: Improvisation* (Pittsburgh, PA: University of Pittsburgh Press, 1994), pp. 36–38, 43.

4. Brian Clark, *Group Theatre* (London: Pitman, 1971), p. 82.

5. Sarah Froeber, *Melvin the Pelican* (Woodstock, IL: Dramatic, 2000).

Deepening the Work

The One-Element-at-a-Time Creative Process

Pick an Element, Any Element

Now you have a structure or organizing principle for your piece and a temporary sequence, or rough draft of a script. How do you turn your rough sketch into a complete, aesthetically pleasing composition?

The best way I know to deepen your piece is to pick one element of composition at a time, work on that element for an hour or so, then ask questions, discuss, and decide about that element. Write down your decisions, so that you know you've progressed and you remember what you did. Then choose another element.

This chapter defines some of the elements of composition and suggests approaches to each one. Read this chapter up through Central Elements; then, when you get lost and don't know how to proceed, glance through Supporting Elements and use them as idea poppers. My list is not exhaustive; add your own with your own exercises.

I am indebted to C. W. Metcalf, corporate trainer from Idyllwild, California, for the one-element-at-a-time approach, which emphasizes process and success. He said,

> Don't wait for brilliant ideas. Nobody comes up with them. Just get to work; pick an element and explore it. Good ideas come from doing things. Put a lot of effort into details of what you have. While you're deciding what kind of watch your character uses, the rest of

Figure 3–1. C. W. Metcalf. Photograph by Joe Coca.

your mind and body will be working on writing the piece. Think about every detail. Try everything—every idea, every which way. If you start with an opening, pick an element and work on details in the opening. Keep working on details; then you will know what follows. Ask questions like, "What works? What can we do with it now?"

You must attack a problem from many different angles. There is no failure in the creative world. There is only process and success. Until you reach success, you are in process, making slow progress.

Don't fret over which element to choose. Look at what you have, and set up an improvisational structure, which will give you more information. Trust your instincts. If you have a gesture, play with it. If you have an atmosphere, create it. If you have text, speak, sing, or move it. If you have a question, devise a way to answer it. You can also use any of the exercises or processes in the first two chapters to move forward from here.

The Web of Composition

An analogy for the one-element-at-a-time process hangs all the elements of composition in a creative spider-web pattern (see Figure 3–2, p. 48). The central idea or image sits in the center of the web. The major elements—concept, logic, structure, audience, statement, design in space and time, and atmosphere—surround the central image on orbital lines closest to the center. The supporting elements hang on orbital lines farther out from the center, near the major element they support.

Just as a spider's movements ripple across its web, changes you make on one element will affect other elements. Clarifying the conflict, for instance, will affect the sequence of events and the characters. Deciding about atmosphere will influence lighting, set, costume, and soundscape. The web of composition connects all the elements.

Central Elements

These seven elements form the inner ring around your initial or central idea: concept, logic, atmosphere, structure, statement, audience, and design in space and time (see Figure 3–3, p. 49).

Concept
The concept is the overarching idea—the gestalt. It includes the world in which the piece takes place. Sartre's *No Exit* gradually reveals its concept that the characters are dead souls discovering the nature of hell. Sometimes a question frames the concept. What if? questions frame the concept for science fiction stories. "What if aliens landed on earth?" Part of the concept for *Star Trek* is, "What happens when humans interact with aliens?"

Concept Statement
Fashioning a concept statement will sharpen your understanding of your concept. A concept statement is a brief series of actions that illustrate or embody the concept. The concept for a TOUCH piece, called *Just One of Those Days*, was that global events affect a

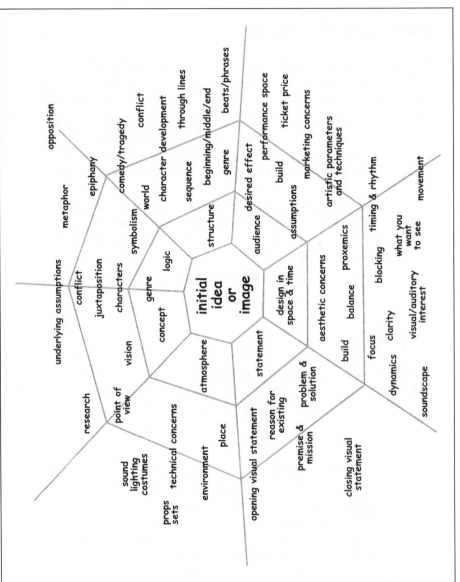

Figure 3–2. The Web of Compositional Elements. Art credit: Steve Durland.

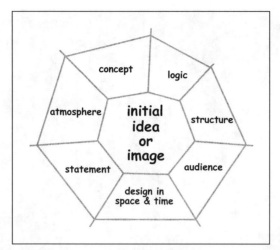

Figure 3–3. The Central Elements of Composition. Art credit: Steve Durland.

character's life, and that her personal actions have global impact (see Figure 3–4). One concept statement might have her throwing out some trash, and then being buried in toxic waste.

After you've crafted a concept statement, craft an opening statement. An opening statement is a brief sequence that pulls in the audience by including the major elements, setting the atmosphere, foreshadowing the conflict, and pointing to the concept of the piece.

Logic

To discover the logic of your piece, ask what rules apply, given the concept of the piece and its world.

The logic of a piece depends on its world. In *Star Trek*, it is logical for the characters to encounter creatures from other planets; not so in Dickens' *A Tale of Two Cities*. In myths, it is logical for animals and gods to talk to humans; not so in realistic dramas. Music, a mood, or a pattern of movement can provide the logic of a dance.

Pick through the piece looking for logic flaws. Ask: What is the next logical step? Where is this headed?

Atmosphere

Atmosphere includes feeling, mood, quality, color, rhythm, time, tone, weather, light, temperature, and weight. Often, when a concept comes to mind, the atmosphere comes with it. Deciding that your

Figure 3–4. Laurie Wolf, Jef, and Sheila Kerrigan in TOUCH Mime Theater's Just One of Those Days. *Photograph by Seth Tice-Lewis.*

piece takes place in a heavy, gray, monotonous atmosphere will facilitate choices about timing, rhythm, and technical ideas.

Atmosphere can inform your choice of genre. A spooky atmosphere may suggest a ghost story; an upbeat atmosphere, a musical comedy. Playing around with improbable atmospheres can twist a piece in interesting ways.

Incorporating Atmosphere

To work on atmosphere, pick one atmospheric quality and invent ways to generate it. Then incorporate it into what you have of the piece. For instance, if you decide on hot, steamy weather, run what you know of the piece and focus on the physical effects of the heat: how your clothes stick to your skin, your hair clings to your face, your thirst increases. Later, focus on the quality of light, then on the emotions the atmosphere generates.

Embodying Atmosphere

Another approach to atmosphere is to embody it. Become the hot, steamy weather. Become the furniture, the plants, the mood, the sounds. Move and talk as they would. Your body will surprise you with what it knows.

Structure

To build a house, you start with the foundation and framework: the footings and two-by-fours onto which you fasten everything else.

In a mystery, the plot provides the structure—the detective discovers a body, uncovers clues, and exposes the murderer. The structure of a performance piece consists of the main events and the bridges between them, without which the piece would fall apart. A dance can rely for its structure on a preexisting form, such as the changing of the seasons, on a musical composition, or on a pattern of movement across the floor. In a dramatic work, a plot and scene outline can define the structure.

Statement

Crafting a pithy statement takes much discussion, but the time invested will prove valuable later. If everyone participates in crafting the statement, and everyone signs on to it, then everyone will commit to the hard work of giving birth to the piece.

A statement is a sentence or paragraph that says what the piece means. Some playwrights include their statement in the dialogue. In Sartre's *No Exit*, Garcin makes the statement, "Hell is other people."[1] Aesop ends each Fable with its statement—the moral of the story—for instance, the race does not always go to the swiftest. The statement is not always a part of the piece; it serves as a tool to focus the creative process. For me, crafting a clear, succinct statement is the most important step in developing a new piece. It holds up a bull's-eye at which all subsequent work aims; it prevents tangential explorations.

Post your statement. Whenever you get stuck making decisions, refer to it for guidance.

Premise and Mission

John O'Neal, formerly of the Free Southern Theatre and now of Junebug Productions in New Orleans, writes a *premise* and a *mission statement:*

> [A] premise is a simple sentence. . . . If you can get it down to three words, that's great. The subject of the sentence is a character, the verb is the action and the object of the sentence is the resolution. . . . In other words, that's a description of the internal order of the piece. "So-and-so's great love conquers all." That's the story you're going to tell. . . . What is the central thing that you're trying to accomplish, stated simply? . . .
>
> There's a larger question for those of us who are concerned with the impact of our work on the world, and that is, what is the relationship of this work . . . to that world? And that brings us backward to the question of mission.
>
> My mission statements normally end up as paragraphs, instead of single sentences, no more than three paragraphs. You try to answer three questions: What is this work about? Who is this work designed for? And, what is the desired result of the work? Or, how do we want the desired audience to be different after they've had this experience than they were before?

Decide how you want to affect your audience; then you will know what works. If you want to shock them, you will make different choices than if you want them feeling warm and fuzzy. Break down your desired effect into its component effects: kinesthetic, emotional, intellectual, and overall.

Audience

Understanding the culture, mores, religion, class, ethnicity, age, and education of your audience will give you genre, language, metaphor, image, references, humor, costume, music—even ticket prices.

Your mission depends on who your audience is. San Francisco's A Traveling Jewish Theatre creates works by, for, and about Jewish Americans. They pepper their text with Yiddish phrases, refer to Jewish traditions, and play traditional music. The Roadside Theater from

Whitesburg, Kentucky, creates works by, for, and about people of the southern Appalachians. Their genre springs from traditional Appalachian storytelling and songs. El Teatro Campesino began as a theater by, for, and about striking Chicano farmworkers. They incorporated the Mexican carpa (tent show), with stock characters, earthy humor, and song and dance.[2]

Design in Space and Time

Pioneering modern dance choreographer Doris Humphrey wrote about design in space and time:

> Design has two aspects: time and space. . . . A dance can be stopped at any moment and it will have a design in space. . . . In addition, there is the design in time, which exists through any moving sequence, lasting from a few seconds to a full-length dance. This . . . ranges from a simple transition of one movement to another— which forms a relationship in time and therefore has a shape—to the lengthier phrase-shape, and finally to the over-all structure.[3]

Play with designs in time by stringing together a series of still shapes. Use images, sounds, or feelings to give you impetus for the shapes. Improvise transitions from one shape to the next to discover a design in time. Your initial idea may contain a design in time: if you start with an idea about birthing and dying, it may lead you to a design in time of rising and falling or spiraling.

Complementary Shapes

Susan Chrietzberg, who teaches theater at the University of Memphis, uses the complementary shapes game to sharpen awareness of design in space. One person makes a shape with his body. A second person makes a shape that relates to the first shape by complementing (completing or perfecting) it. The first person steps away and looks at the second shape. A third person then makes a shape that relates to and complements the second shape. The second person steps out and looks at the new shape, then a new person makes a complementary shape.

First Variation: Make an opposing shape instead of a complementary one.

Second Variation: Choose to make either a complementary or an opposing shape.

Supporting Elements

At any point in your creative process you can explore any element. Use the following supporting elements to help figure out what to work on next.

World

Define the world in which the piece takes place. Does the logic of that world hold sway throughout? How do you communicate the world to your audience? What information does the world give you about sound, movement, language, costumes, props, set pieces, lighting, and characters? Some worlds to choose from include

- the world of myths: the kachina ceremonies of the Rio Grande Pueblo peoples
- the world of symbolism, where objects and people stand for other things: medieval European morality plays
- Limbo: Beckett's "Waiting for Godot"
- Heaven: parts of the Indian epic *Ramayana*
- Hell, or the underworld: Dante's *Inferno*
- the world inside our minds; the world of how we feel about things: the fantasy sequences in the movie *American Beauty*
- the real world, of which the audience is a part: clowns and street performers
- the world where anything can happen: Blue Man Group's *Tubes.*
- the dream world: the works of Black Light Theatre of Prague
- another planet: science fiction
- the world of TV
- an ideal world: B. F. Skinner's *Walden Two*

Underlying Assumptions

Talk about what you take for granted in the world you wish to create, and what the audience must understand. If you refer to historic or futuristic events, how much does your audience know about them, and how much do they need to know to understand your piece? Does your work hold a political slant? Does your audience share it?

Symbolism

If you use symbols, know what stands for what. Do your symbols call to mind the things they stand for? Follow each symbol through the piece, checking consistency: does it mean the same thing throughout? Consider whether the weight, tone, and size of your movement, language, and set match those of the symbolic world.

Ritual

In some Christian churches the priest eats a wafer and drinks wine in a ritual repetition of the Last Supper, which symbolizes the redemption of sinners through the sacrifice of Jesus.

Rituals are actions that, through repetition and symbolism, carry more meaning within their social context than the actions alone carry. Rituals appear in works of performing art because they contain a natural order and beauty. If you use a ritual, what function does it fulfill?

Beware of co-opting rituals from a culture that you do not understand. Audience members may feel that you are cheapening or ripping off their cultural heritage. On the other hand, respectful and judicious use of a ritual known to you and your audience can have a powerful effect.

Conflict

Since before Aristotle wrote *Poetics*, conflict has provided the crux of European-based drama. A protagonist wants something and struggles against obstacles that prevent him from getting it. A hero struggles against the forces of evil and, in a tragedy, is defeated. Define your conflict and its resolution.

Opposition

If your piece involves two opposing forces (good versus evil, individual courage versus a cowardly community), explore their impact on each other. Chart the conflict between them across time, marking which force dominates when. Clarify how one wins dominance over the other.

Walk through what you have while following the dynamics of the opposition, highlighting moments when the balance changes. These

T034359

moments contain heightened dramatic tension or comedy. They inform you about structure and build.

Epiphany

Saint Paul, on his way to Damascus to persecute Jesus' followers, was blinded by ". . . a light out of heaven: and he fell upon the earth, and heard a voice saying unto him, Saul, Saul, why persecutest thou Me?"[4] This epiphany of Saint Paul transformed him from a persecutor of Christians to a Christian missionary.

The epiphanic moment occurs when the main character finally "gets it"; when his worldview flip-flops. Oedipus' epiphanies come when he discovers that he killed his father and married his mother. The audience can experience an epiphany when they grasp what is happening, their "Aha!" The epiphany can occur at the climax or it can happen offstage, in which case the protagonist might re-enter and describe his revelation.

Construct an epiphanic moment: a brief episode that contains the turning point.

Juxtaposition

Juxtaposing unrelated ideas, events, or things together to create an effect that is bigger than the sum of the parts can propel a piece from the ordinary to the striking. TV commercials exploit the juxtaposition of unrelated elements. They flash pictures of a beach, a mountaintop, a woman's body, and a car. The car bears no relationship to the beach, mountain, or woman, but it derives a certain cachet from its proximity to the other images.

René Magritte mastered the use of juxtaposing unrelated images, painting a sky inside the space of a man's head, for example. Much humor derives from unlikely combinations—"Jesus, Mohammed, and Buddha are playing golf. . . ."

If you use juxtaposition, discuss how you want it to affect your meaning. What does it signify? How do the combination of elements twist reality? Clarify the relationships between the parts.

Comedy

Do you mean to be funny? Are you funny enough? Bill Allard of Duck's Breath Mystery Theater talked about what makes something funny.

You don't try to "be funny." Comedy is the juxtaposition of ideas that people haven't seen before. A lot of what we did involved putting together bizarre ideas, connecting them. Like, *Gonad, the Barbarian. The Duck of the Baskervilles. MacScout: the MacBeth Tragedy Takes Place at Scout Camp.* You know how serious *MacBeth* is, and how serious scout camp is: you combine the two and the seriousness of the two makes the juxtaposition work.

Comedy is just surprise. The better you are as a writer and actor, the better you are at being funny. When we were working on a western, we had all the standard characters, only there's this astronaut. That's it: OK, that's funny, that's weird, if you can fit it in correctly, that's comedy.

Point of View

Writers call the point of view the narrative voice. The audience identifies with the character who embodies the point of view.

Sometimes the central character provides the point of view, as Dorothy does in *The Wizard of OZ*. Sometimes a narrator gives the point of view, as does teacher James Leeds in Mark Medoff's play, *Children of a Lesser God*. A piece can be told from the point of view of the dead, a god, a thousand-year-old, or a three-year-old. The point of view feeds you information about elements like size, conflict, language, and movement.

Is the point of view of your piece consistent? If it changes, clarify when and how. If the central character begins young and ends old, how do her language and movement develop? If the point of view switches from one character to another, do you communicate the switch clearly?

Characters

Sometimes a character springs to life whole and forms a center for a piece, like Athena from the brow of Zeus. In that case, let your character help write the piece.

Play with your character. Take her out to bars, restaurants, churches, parks. Find out how she interacts with the world. Ask her about her family and childhood. Let her tell stories. Write it all down.

When you do not start with a character, construct one based on what you know of her actions and whatever text you have written. Many books map out avenues to follow in search of a character.[5]

Examine every shred of information in the given words and actions of both your main character and the others, and draw logical and psychological conclusions about their motivations, needs, and wants. Approaches to developing a character include motivation, physicalization, internal world, emotional subtext, and negotiation over objects.

What the Actors Know

Your actors can inform you about your writing. Places that seem awkward from the actor's point of view need to be examined from the writer's. If a competent actor cannot justify an action her character takes, look for a flaw in the writing.

Motivation

I learned an enlightening script analysis method from Beth Skinner, who was a student of Paul Gray at Bennington College. I write down every action my character takes on one side of a page. Opposite each action I write a sentence that begins, "I want," "I need," or "I must." If my action is "to shake hands with the governor," my sentence could be, "I must tell him about my little boy." Or, "I must not be photographed." My objective (or motivation) colors how I perform the action.

Physicalization

Every individual has a unique repertoire of body language and nonverbal communication. Studying these elements can offer another ingress to character.

Nonverbal communication includes voice, breath, intonation, diction, dialect, and tempo, as well as energy and emotion. Investigate and practice the nonverbal communication of your characters. Your investigation will affect timing, dynamics, build, relationships, and blocking.

Body language includes observable movements, postures, facial expressions, and gestures. Body language study involves trying on movement patterns different from your own; it gets the emotional juices flowing. Each aspect of body language that you incorporate will change the way you feel and think. Here are some aspects of body language.[6]

- relationship to earth and sky: Is she grounded? Does she float?
- rhythm: sing your character's rhythm; move in her rhythm.
- quantity of movement: How much does she move? Which parts move a lot, and which move little?
- quality of movement: Is it tense or relaxed, hard or soft, direct or indirect, slow or fast?[7] Which parts of the body move with which qualities?
- relationship between parts of the body: Where does she touch herself? Where is she connected? where disconnected? Where does tension block ease of movement?
- energy: Where is it? what kind, what color? like what substance? Where does it flow? Where is it blocked?
- carriage, posture: What is the shape of the body?
- relationship to space: Does she knife through space? ooze through it? fill it up? try to disappear in it?
- proxemics: Proxemics is the study of how bodies use space. How much space does she need for comfort? What are her cultural proxemics norms?
- characteristic gestures: What specific movements does she make when she is angry, happy, sad, scared, lying?
- sexuality: How would you describe her sexual energy?
- sensuality: What does she feel? What does she love to feel? What disgusts her?
- age: How has time affected her body? What effect have past experiences, work, accidents, had on her body?

Internal World

Investigate your character's inner world. Try using similes: Her emotional life is like a roller coaster, or a slug. Her attitude is like a puppy's. She feels like a heavy metal band. She thinks like a computer, or like fireworks. The image exercises in Chapter 2 will help you to find and incorporate similes into your character. Let each image affect you as you improvise scenes.

The aural equivalent of image exercises can tap into vocal qualities. Close your eyes and listen to your character speak and sing in your imagination. Speak as you hear her speak. Let your voice follow hers accurately.

The voice and body forge direct links to emotions. If you move the way a character moves and speak in her voice, you will draw out her feelings and place them in the space.

Emotional Subtext

Liz Lerman, of Liz Lerman Dance Exchange, Takoma Park, Maryland, has a way of working from feelings to movement, which she calls "emotional subtext":

> A lot of the attempt of my work is to separate for a while from the feeling so you can explore fully and totally kinesthetically, with intellectual and creative curiosity. Let's say I tell you a story about saying good-bye to my daughter. . . . I'm really sad, and we hug each other a lot. She ran away across a bridge, and then she came back and hugged me. . . . There is an emotion there, an incredible grief about having to part. So I might isolate or separate the question of grief and turn it into its effect on the body. I might hunch my shoulders, for instance, or have a pain in my tummy and bend over. I might spend a whole day messing around with trying to find a phrase where my shoulders are curved and I am bent over, with my back curved. I wouldn't even be thinking about grief. . . . Then I might do that phrase while telling the story.
>
> It's kind of neat to curve your spine and see how many ways you can move, but if I'm feeling sad, I would never try that, because when you're feeling sad, you don't turn in circles and jump up and down. . . . Once you have gone through this process, it's really powerful when you reconnect with the feeling.

Characters Negotiating

Jeffrey Sweet, New York playwright and author of *The Dramatist's Toolkit*, said:

> If you can't analyze a scene as a negotiation, you don't have a scene. . . . *Othello* is three characters negotiating over a handkerchief. Macbeth negotiates for a crown; Lear negotiates for a home. . . . Sometimes characters negotiate over an object, sometimes over a person or a space.

Sweet recommends improvising with two characters who each have an object of importance over which they negotiate. Choosing a meaningful object can clarify a character, concretize relationships, and give a piece a visual thread.

Relationships Between Characters

Chart the development of the relationships between characters over time. Know each character's status in relationship to the others and when their status changes.

Blocking

Modern dance trailblazer Doris Humphrey described the stage as "a sensitive musical instrument to play on."[8]

Humphrey mapped out the meaning of positions and directions on stage. A cross from stage right to stage left can convey the passage of time. The up-right-to-down-left diagonal is the strongest. Down center implies confrontation with the audience in the present time, including comedy. Upstage implies tragedy. Humphrey cautioned that the power of any spot on stage diminishes with overuse.[9]

Blocking, or who goes where, and when, sheds light on relationship, status, and motivation. Where you go, who you face, and how your position relates to others all carry meaning. As you block, know how each body relates to the others. Ask what it means, how it feels, that these bodies go here or there. Try a run-through with the actors going wherever their impulses move them as they improvise. Make a floor-pattern diagram of everybody's movements, then analyze the positions in terms of the piece.

Protagonist and Chorus

Jacques LeCoq, who taught performance arts in Paris, used the following exercise, based on ancient Greek drama's protagonist and chorus format, to teach students about the dynamics of a stage picture. Endow a space on the floor with the quality of a raft afloat. The first person to step onto the space plays the protagonist—the main character. He represents a larger-than-life figure, a god or a king. He goes wherever he wishes on the raft. The next person, who plays the chorus, steps onto it without upsetting the balance. The chorus keeps the raft even by counterbalancing the protagonist's every move. Each newcomer who steps onto the raft joins the chorus, and moves only in relation to the protagonist. The chorus, no matter how many people it comprises, weighs the same as the protagonist. Whenever the protagonist moves, the chorus counterbalances him. If he moves toward one corner, they move toward the opposite. If he moves to the center, they spread out evenly around him.

Variations: have two protagonists, or split the chorus, or allow for revolution, where a member of the chorus vies with the protagonist for his position.

Choreography

Choreography, or composition and arrangement of movement, involves many elements; here are some that you can use to shape your piece.[10]

- dimension or plane: Every movement describes a line or a plane. Are you aware of the lines and planes you are creating?
- direction of movement: Does the direction of movement reinforce your meaning?
- focus of the movement: Which is the most important part?
- relationship between positive and negative space in shaping: Can you use the air as negative space, which you sculpt with your body?
- tempo and rhythm: Do you use a monotonous beat? Can you vary it? What movements do you want to accent?
- repeated movements: How many and to what effect?
- energy and force: Can you vary the intensity, strength, and quality of your movements?
- form: Does your choreography have a strict form like a piece of music, for example, round, theme and variation, Rondo (ABACADA)? Can you borrow forms from natural cycles—the seasons, day and night?
- motif manipulation: Can you vary a movement phrase? Do it faster, higher, lower? Round it, square it, jump it, fall it, slide it, roll it? Change direction, force, emotion, or do it with a different part?
- economy of movement: Can you do more with less? How much is enough?
- cumulative effect: Does it add up to what you want?
- technique and performer safety: Are you executing it well? Can you repeat it many times without injury?
- the movement's meaning and its relationship to the statement: Does it contribute? Does it clarify your meaning?

Physicalization of Psychological States

Barbara Vann, who directs New York's Medicine Show Theatre Ensemble, invents physical exercises to reveal her characters' relationships and internal states. She described the exercises as "physicalizations of the problem in the theater piece. So that the [actor] experiences it viscerally or kinetically, rather than intellectually. . . . [The exercises] are interesting when they are paradigms for life."

To explore the relationship between a dependent character and a supportive one, she might ask the actors to move together in ways that neither of them could move individually. They might do a wheelbarrow, or one could drag the other. Physicalizations concretize the reality underlying the text.

Movement Metaphors

Liz Lerman talked about movement metaphors. She recalled the story of saying good-bye to her daughter.

> I'm curious what's inside that story that could be a movement metaphor. Well, one of the movement metaphors is just the verb: running away and coming back. So I might set up an improvisational structure that's all about running away and coming back. All we would do would be to explore, not emotionally, but physically, kinesthetically, and intellectually, all the ways you can run away and come back. My arms running away from me and coming back to my body. My body running away from the space and coming back in. Working in pairs, working alone, whatever. So that when I tell the story, what you would see physically might be my arms running away from me and coming back to the center of my body. That's an example of a movement metaphor.

Movement Phrases

A movement phrase is the "smallest and simplest unit of form. It is a short but complete unit in that it has a beginning, middle, and end."[11]

Each phrase has a structure, with a high or low point. Break down your movement into phrases. Work out how to do each phrase with focus and intention. How does each phrase connect to its preceding and following phrases? String two or three phrases together, focusing on their relationships and transitions. Repeat this investigation with groups of two or three phrases, then string several phrase groups together with transitions. Keep increasing the number of phrase combinations and work on the transitions.

Timing and Rhythm

Timing concerns when each action occurs and how long each action takes. Rhythm is the rate of speed at which a series of actions takes place. Comedy moves faster than tragedy. Investigate the timing and duration of each phrase. Articulate the speech and movement patterns. Explore how emotions affect timing, and how the rhythm contributes to build. Run a speech or movement sequence while players vocalize the rhythms of their parts. How much and how little time do you need to get the main point of each section across? Does repetition strengthen the impact? Write and execute a rhythm score for the piece, using tempo, meter, and beat to emphasize or downplay aspects of your characters or your plot.

Dynamics

The word *dynamic* stems from the Greek word for power. Dynamics include variations in stress, volume, energy, force, size, speed, direction, rhythm, the equilibrium of parts, and the quality of movement.

Vocalize the dynamics of a dance. Dance the dynamics of a text. Build the dynamics to boost the climax. Exaggerate the dynamic changes. Draw a diagram of the dynamics of the whole.

You can describe sound, text, movement, structure, and action in terms of musical dynamics. Use words like the following:

- *legato*   smooth, connected, flowing
- *staccato*   crisp, short notes separated by silences
- *pizzicato*   plucked, short notes separated by silence
- *dolce*   sweetly
- *crescendo*   growing louder
- *crescendo il tempo*   growing faster
- *diminuendo*   growing quieter
- *diminuendo il tempo*   growing slower
- *piano, pianissimo*   quietly, very quietly
- *forte, fortissimo*   loudly, very loudly
- *accent*   emphasis or force

- *mute*   muffle, deaden
- *counterpoint*   independent, interwoven voices
- *beat*   the basis of rhythm
- *monotone*   one note played continuously or repeated
- *rest*   silent space between sounds[12]

Visual and Aural Statements

Images and sounds create visual and aural statements. Here are some questions to ask to maximize your use of these elements. What is the most compelling visual image? How can we strengthen the impact with sound and light? How can we graphically portray this?

Examine your opening visual and aural statements. What do they say? What do they promise? Do they prepare the audience for what follows? How do they relate to the rest of the piece?

Think about the final image and sounds. How do they relate to what precedes them? Do they wrap it up? Do they leave things dangling? Do they add a twist? Do you want to leave the audience resonating with those images and sounds?

Do the visual and aural effects intensify your impact? Is the cumulative effect larger than the parts?

Graphics

Tony Montanaro uses the word *graphic* to mean an arresting visual image created by bodies and/or objects in motion that calls to mind the real thing. A graphic communicates the essence of a thing instantly.

To make a graphic, you can use bodies alone, or you can combine bodies with props, set or costume pieces, masks, slides, sound, film, video, color, or light. You can also use those elements without any bodies. In Alvin Ailey's dance "Revelations," dancers create a graphic of a river by spreading long blue and white cloths across the width of the stage and shaking the ends so ripples flow across the stage.

Visual and Verbal Clarity

Test your piece for comprehensibility. Can you get the point across more succinctly, more poetically, with more punch? Blocking, phrasing, and proxemics affect the clarity. What are the clearest movements, words, images, and sounds that will communicate your meaning?

Focus

Focus aids clarity. Focus means three things: where you want the performers to look; where you want the audience to look; and what you want the audience to hear.

The performers can focus inward, without making eye contact with others on stage or in the audience; they can focus in the middle distance, making eye contact with fellow performers and the audience; or they can focus in the far distance, seeing through walls and past the horizon. People in daily life switch from one distance to another all the time.[13] Run through your piece and articulate where the performers focus.

If you have ten people on stage, the audience can see and hear only one person or group at a time. Understanding where you want the focus to be informs the blocking and spotlights the important action. Your audience will gladly follow your lead if your focus is clear.

Hocus-Pocus, Who's Got the Focus? In TOUCH, we played "Hocus-Pocus, Who's Got the Focus?" We ran through a scene with each actor saying, "I have the focus. I'm sharing the focus with you. We have the focus. I'm giving the focus to you," at the appropriate moments. Anytime two actors said, "I have the focus" at once, we would stop and find out whether we wanted shared focus or just had a muddle. We timed the moments of focus exchange precisely. We passed focus back and forth, to implant the moment-to-moment dance of the focus into our bodies.

Use a ball to concretize focus in a muddy scene. Whoever has the focus plays with the ball. He tosses it when he gives focus to someone else. When two players share focus, they toss the ball back and forth between them.

Beat-to-Beat

Beats are the actor's equivalent of movement phrases. A beat is something happening: a small sequence with a beginning, a middle, and an end in which everything moves in one direction.

A beat can end when a character learns something, feels something, or changes something. Obvious ends-of-beats are exits, faints, deaths, and punch lines. Obvious beginnings-of-beats are entrances, revelations, decisions, and strong actions. Many beats are small. A sigh might mark an ending. A beat may begin with the beginning of a kiss, and end at the end of the kiss. Or the kiss may break out into two beats, the first beat tentative, the second, committed and with gusto.

Breaking down your piece to its beats tells you about structure, rhythm, build, detail, timing, the subtlety of emotions, and the development of relationships.

Technical Concerns
Even though technical concerns are the last of this list of elements, don't wait till the end of your process to consider sound, lighting, costumes, props, and running the backstage. A prop, mask, musical composition, or costume can act like a seed for your creative process. Joan Schirle, coartistic director of The Dell'Arte Company in Blue Lake, California, said,

> We very much believe in the collaboration of designers with us. We don't, if possible, hand a finished piece to a designer and say, "Design this." . . . A creative team doesn't just consist of writers and actors; designers are a major part of that team. . . . [Our designer] cowrote two plays with us. . . . He always contributed ideas about the play, about the acting, about other areas. We consider him as much a collaborator as we are, and respect his judgment.

All these elements of composition look like a lot of work. Don't despair. No single group works on every element. The list is like all the possible ingredients for a soup—you don't have to use everything. Pick what appeals to you and suits your needs.

Add to this list of elements whatever elements you use, and ignore whatever doesn't apply. Each time you explore a new element, you are lifting the top of a soup pot and tossing in a new ingredient which will affect the soup. Take a taste. Look at the whole, and ask how you have changed it by what you have just done.

Each change will provoke new questions. The questions are a spoon stirring up ingredients on the bottom of the pot. Keep asking questions (see Chapter Two) and you will discover the next logical step in your creative process. Good questions drive good creative work.

Notes

1. Jean-Paul Sartre, *No Exit*, in *No Exit and Three Other Plays* (New York: Vintage Books, 1956), p. 47.

2. Yolanda Broyles-González, *El Teatro Campesino: Theater in the Chicano Movement* (Austin, TX: University of Texas Press, 1994), p. 10.

3. Doris Humphrey, *The Art of Making Dances*, edited by Barbara Pollack (New York: Rinehart and Company, 1959), p. 49.

4. Acts 9.3-4 American Standard Version.

5. Constantin Stanislavski, *Building a Character* translated by Elizabeth Reynolds Hapgood (New York: Theatre Arts Books, 1977), and *Creating a Role*, translated by Elizabeth Reynolds Hapgood (New York: Theatre Arts Books, 1961); Uta Hagen, *Respect for Acting* (New York: Macmillan, 1973); Stella Adler, *The Technique of Acting* (Toronto and New York: Bantam Books, 1988).

6. I learned body language analysis from C. W. Metcalf at the Magic Mountain Mime School. Useful books include Edward T. Hall, *The Silent Language* (Garden City, NY: Anchor/Doubleday, 1973), and *Beyond Culture* (Garden City, NY: Anchor/Doubleday, 1977); Nancy M. Henley, *Body Politics: Power, Sex, and Nonverbal Communication* (Englewood Cliffs, NJ: Prentice-Hall, 1977); Cecily Dell, *A Primer for Movement Description Using Effort-Shape and Supplementary Concepts* (New York: Dance Notation Bureau Press, 1977).

7. Rudolf Laban and F. C. Lawrence, *Effort*, 2d ed. (Plymouth, England: MacDonald and Evans, 1974).

8. Humphrey, p. 82.

9. Ibid., pp. 72–90.

10. I am indebted to Lynne Anne Blom and L. Tarin Chaplin, *The Intimate Act of Choreography* (Pittsburgh, PA: University of Pittsburgh Press, 1982), pp. 24–95, for the elements of choreography.

11. Ibid., p. 23.

12. *Music Lovers' Encyclopedia*, revised and edited by Deems Taylor and Russell Kerr from materials compiled by Rupert Hughes (Garden City, NY: Doubleday, 1954).

13. Joyce Morgenroth, *Dance Improvisations* (Pittsburgh, PA: University of Pittsburgh Press, 1987), pp. 27–28.

4 Organizing Your Material, Getting Stuck, and Cutting

By now you've hit upon an idea, researched it, made some decisions about its shape and structure, and approached it from numerous angles using the one-element-at-a-time process.

This chapter offers practical ways for your group to envision your piece in a field that all can see. It suggests ways to write a script or text collaboratively. It deals with a recurring moment in the creative process—when you get stuck—and presents antidotes. And it encourages you to have the courage to cut when you have created too much. You may need this chapter earlier in your process if you amass a ton of material quickly. You can get stuck on day one, or any day. You may start writing scenes as soon as you choose an idea. Pop into this chapter as the need arises.

Some Physical Ways to Organize Material

To track your progress: get all the information about your piece into one place, an area where everybody can see it, point to it, talk about it, manipulate it, and organize it. Cover the walls with paper and write everything you know about the piece on the walls. Make changes on the walls as you change the piece.

Use the Wall for Everything: Provisional Theatre

Director Steven Kent recalled that Provisional Theatre used to divide up areas of interest; for instance, speeches, stories, music, history, and research. Each individual had expertise in his or her own area, but nobody knew everything. They centralized their knowledge on a blank wall. Everything went on the wall: ideas, themes, conceptions, speeches, songs. Everybody could see it, and could envision the whole. "You keep it in a field, and just arrange it so everybody has a sense of it. Then the ideas talk back to you," Kent said.

Arrange Post-it® Notes: Steven Kent

When Steven Kent guest-directed TOUCH, he showed us how to use Post-it® Notes to organize our material and rough out scenes. Here's how it works: along the top of a big piece of paper stick a note for each main character or major element. Each time the protagonist, for example, experiences a change (an "aha!" or major action) write the change on a note and stick it in the vertical column under the protagonist's name. So if you read vertically down his column, you can follow his development from scene to scene. If each of the protagonist's major changes marks a scene, you can create a horizontal row

Figure 4–1. Steven Kent

next to each of his major changes with Post-it Notes that delineate what happens with other characters and important elements in that scene. Place those notes under their respective columns, so you can chart each main character's development vertically and each scene's major points horizontally.

Post the outline on the studio wall. Whenever you make changes, keep track by rearranging the Post-it Notes.

Kent, as we fleshed out scenes, used a binder, with one page for each scene and a little Post-it Note for each action, and arranged them so that each character had a column on the page (see Figure 4–2). Two characters involved two columns; three characters involved three, and so on. For technical rehearsals, he made columns on the opposite page for prop and set changes and for lighting and sound effects.

Write on the Blackboard: Stageworks Touring Company

Carolyn O'Donnell was founder and producing artistic director of Stageworks Touring Company in Glassboro, New Jersey. They received a grant to produce a play, based on interviews, about the dwindling number of family farms in their region. O'Donnell initially conducted library research, "to insure that the questions we asked were informed and pertinent and, so, respectful of the nature of the informants' work and time."

The actors visited seventy-five farms, set up tape recorders in kitchens, barns, greenhouses, or fields, and interviewed farming families. After transcribing pertinent sections of the interview tapes, they wrote the major themes and metaphors on a blackboard. For each theme, they searched the transcripts for clear passages, and used the passages as platforms from which to improvise. The playwright then wrote scenes using the improvs and portions of some interviews verbatim. Threads emerged that tied together the different scenes and the actors used them to unite the scenes into a coherent whole.

List What You'd Like to See: Five Lesbian Brothers

New York's Five Lesbian Brothers discuss what they'd like to see in their piece. They make a list of all the things they want: characters, scenes, lines, action, images, songs, and places. When they get lost in the creative process, somebody says, "Let's look at the list."

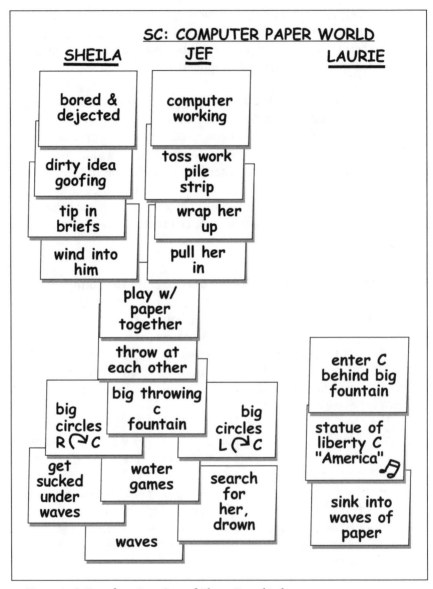

Figure 4–2. Page from Just One of Those Days *binder*

Shuffle Cards on the Floor: Adam Gertsacov

Clown and director Adam Gertsacov's master's thesis in Theatre and Communications at Rhode Island College involved forming a group to create a performance piece titled *The One Sure Thing: A Cabaret on Death*. The group wrote thirty-five sketches on death and dying. When the time came to order them, he wrote the title of each one on a separate card and scattered the cards across the floor. They played with different orders by moving the cards around.

They grouped similar sketches together, and tossed the weaker ones into a reject pile. They pulled out to the sides ones that would function as opening and closing sketches. Some choices depended on which actors would do which sketches and how much time they needed to change from one sketch to the next; other choices came from a desire for varied dynamics and mood. They chose some to make bridges between others, and some to provide a through line.

Videotape It: TOUCH

Videotaping what you have can give you a sense of its shape, and of what is missing. The monitor shows an objective view without comment. It helps performers gain distance and objectify their work. If something doesn't work, it's hard to deny it when you see it in front of you. A camera can reduce the amount of argument over which way to play a scene. You can try it each way, tape the trials, and the video tells you. If you improvise verbally, audiotapes preserve your brilliant lines for transcription, and listening to the tapes clarifies the story.

Show a Storyboard: Bloomsburg Theatre Ensemble

A storyboard looks like a big comic strip and acts like a pictorial outline. Videographers make a storyboard by laying out a series of pictures that show the major shots.

Company member Leigh Strimbeck learned about storyboarding from Ann Bogart and brought it to Pennsylvania's Bloomsburg Theatre Ensemble. They make a storyboard with their bodies, by inventing a series of still pictures or sculptures that encapsulate the story of the piece. To show the series, an actor calls out "blackout," the observers close their eyes, and the actors get into position. Then the actor says, "lights" and the observers open their eyes to see the still picture. The process is repeated for each still picture.

Having a mechanism to view your material as it grows and evolves is vital. Whether you use cards on the floor, butcher paper on the wall, drawings, recordings, or a computer, anything that helps you envision the whole will help clarify the piece.

Some Ways to Write Collaboratively

Here are some methods groups use to write text or a script collaboratively.

To the Woods: The Dell'Arte Company

Joan Schirle, coartistic director of The Dell'Arte Company in Blue Lake, California, talked about their evolving writing process. To begin a new work, they go on retreat for several days of intense, uninterrupted writing—ideally in a cabin in the woods.

I Write My Scene, You Write Yours

At first, everyone had a hand in writing everything. If Schirle wrote a scene, someone else could change it. But Schirle noted, "If you are going to use words at all, you probably choose them carefully. Your style loses coherence if someone else changes what you write." They agreed to determine the themes, characters, and scenarios together, and then to each write certain scenes alone, with the original writer making new drafts based on group feedback. This has proved more effective.

Computer Director

Once they draft a script, they return to the studio for script-in-hand rehearsals, where changes happen rapidly. In the flow of reading and improvising, better ideas come up. To keep track, an assistant director sits at a computer, notating changes as they happen. Each day she hands out the latest version of the script. She also skillfully mediates arguments over changes.

To Each His Own: Pomo Afro Homos

Djola Branner, a founder and former performer with Pomo Afro Homos (Postmodern African American Homosexuals) in San Francisco, said,

> We each went about writing either ensemble work or solo work in the privacy of our own homes, at our own desks. And then we

would come together for rehearsals, and that's when the material would be workshopped. . . . Once we got the scripts in hand and were standing up and moving things around, the lines would change, or someone would have a particular suggestion of how to make a certain line work. . . . Those types of things would happen, but the author would always be given full credit for authoring the skit.

Mouse Control: Cornerstone Theater Company

David Reiffel was a composer with Cornerstone Theater Company for their first five years. They adapted classical plays to contemporary times and local situations. They had the complete works of Shakespeare on computer disk. As few as three, or as many as nine writers clustered around the computer. Reiffel said,

> We talk about it a lot. People are throwing out suggestions. Sometimes people would say, "Ooo, let me try this," and everyone will stand back and they'll just type something in, and then it will get adjusted. There tended to be a real driver's seat mentality. Whoever had the mouse on the computer had the power. . . . Trying to tell it to whoever was sitting at the keyboard in order for them to type it in became really frustrating, and we'd say, "Just give me the keyboard, and let me type it in." . . . There was lots of going back to the original, trying to pick it apart and really trying to figure out what it is doing to get the equivalent. . . .
>
> [Conflicting ideas] would coexist for a long time. . . . We would often have these totally incoherent documents with version A, version B. . . . When we cut something out, instead of getting rid of it, we would put it at the end of the document, so that it was still there for reference in case we got into a blind alley and had to back up a few steps.

Talk to Me: Howling Woolf Theatre

Jyl Hewston wrote, acted, and directed with Howling Woolf Theatre in Arcata, California, in the 1990s. She said they got together to brainstorm.

> "What's the point we want to make? What scenes do we want? What characters do we need?" Then I go off and do some writing with one other person. We'll sit at the kitchen table, and I'll say, "What if the aerobics instructor does this?" My writing partner will

respond as the character, and just speak in character. Then I'll respond in character. Then we'll write it down and continue on.

All Contribute, One Writes

Both the Stageworks Touring Company in Glassboro, New Jersey, and the Dakota Theatre Caravan assigned one person the ultimate responsibility for unifying the contributions of company members. Everyone, including actors and musicians, gathers material by improvising, researching, interviewing, writing, composing, choreographing, or developing characters; one person, the keeper of the vision, or the best writer or director, gleans and combines to make a script.

When You Get Stuck

Dead Horse

The creative process includes frustrating times, when you work hard and get nowhere. You try one solution after another; they all bomb. Frustration mounts; you're talking through clenched teeth. It's time to lie on your back and stick your arms and legs up in the air—the sign for a dead horse. It's time to quit.

When you get stuck, you are on the verge of discovery, but you won't find it by beating the dead horse. Leave the problem. Your subconscious mind needs time to mull it over. The subconscious knows everything we ever knew and remembers every experience. It knows nothing of logic, censorship, judgment, or morals. It creates illogical connections, digs up forgotten material. It provides us with original ideas.

Some Ways to Get Unstuck

I asked everyone I interviewed what they do when they get stuck. Here are some answers:

Jef: Sleeping on the Job

Try going to sleep when you get stuck. My partner in TOUCH, Jef, dreams solutions to creative problems.

When I'm stuck, I define the problem in my mind and take a short nap. I often wake up fifteen minutes later with a solution.

C. W. Metcalf: Work on an Unrelated Element

C. W. Metcalf said, "Drop whatever you are doing and work on an unrelated element. If you can't figure out a transition between two sections, forget it. Go build some props, or have a business meeting."

Andrew Long, Johnson/Long Dance Company: Coffee and Doughnuts

"Go Home. Go out for coffee and doughnuts."

Tom Keegan and Davidson Lloyd: Look Under Your Nose

Davidson Lloyd uses dancer/choreographer Daniel Nagrin's advice: return to your original image and emotion for inspiration when you're stuck.

Tom Keegan said,

> Very often we get stuck because we aren't in the moment. We ought to look at that very moment, what's right there, and what wants to happen in that time. Whatever we're trying, "What's going on right now?" We think we have to look far away. It's right under our noses.

TOUCH: Hat Tricks

One time TOUCH got completely stuck on a piece for a symphony performance. We each stewed: I sat in the corner, company member Laurie Wolf paced, Jef practiced hat tricks. After twenty minutes, we gave up and went home, discouraged. Next day Wolf came in with a solution involving hat tricks.

Darby Hayes: Listen to Self-Talk

Darby Hayes performs and teaches collaboration skills to professionals throughout South Florida. She says:

> Someone's coming up with a block. They don't know where to go from here. To cut through that cement block with a laser beam would be to ask, "What am I saying to myself right now?" Whatever we are saying to ourselves is standing in the way of moving in some direction. The self-talk might be: "I'm not enough right here, right now. I can't do it. They're better than me. I'm less than. . . ." So either you're calling down on yourself, or you're negatively criticizing the other, which is usually a projection of your own limitations.

Keith Hennessy, Contraband: Do Anything

Keith Hennessy performs with San Francisco's anarchist-inspired collective, Contraband. When they get stuck, he said, they try a different tack, switch media, work with props, do visualization, do voice and sound work. He continued,

> We'll do anything, I mean, when I was blocked with Sara [Shelton Mann, the artistic director], I refused to come to rehearsal unless it was after midnight and [we all came] with no clothes on. "Oh, and no talking," I said. "Until we do that, I'm not coming to rehearsal. I need a totally different environment." We were all mad with each other, and everyone would say, "You're being manipulative. . . . I'm not coming to rehearsal." Sara was the only one [who came]. We had a rehearsal and made incredible material, which ended up in the next show.
>
> The other thing we do is we go outside, or we just come to the studio and meditate. . . . Or we hire someone to come teach us a new skill.

Steven Kent: Table It

Director Steven Kent has thirty years of collaborative writing experience. He's learned to relax, and not get upset.

> I usually table it. Don't get anxious or fuss. . . . Sometimes I just go, "OK, I've done everything I can on this particular issue." Put it aside, and not think about it. I can let my unconscious work on it. And sometimes the unconscious will wake me up in the middle of the night, two or four days later, and go, "Have you thought of this?" You can't resent your unconscious because it has no sense of time. That's why I keep a pad of paper near my bed most of the time. Because some knotty problems need to be worked out on unconscious levels. . . .
>
> Or, I'll just accept it, even all the way into production, or even through production. "I didn't figure that out. I don't know what to do with that." . . .
>
> And then, sometimes you just have to confront it because it's too ugly. "This actor can't do this. They gotta be fired." Or, "This person has to stop doing this now." . . .
>
> Joe Chaikin would say, "Turn it into a question." Then he'd say, "I'll go home and give it a good think; and I'll come back with a question."

Joseph Chaikin wrote about The Open Theatre's 1968 production. "There are many things in *The Serpent* which are still unsolved—in fact, I don't remember being part of any ambitious work which has seemed to me solved."[1]

Gerard Stropnicky, Bloomsburg Theatre Ensemble: Do Alexander

We do Alexander [Technique] on each other. Often, if especially we are working very closely on a play and things aren't working, we'll just get together and massage each other, Alexander each other for a while. That's been very helpful. Take an hour to do that, and you've released things in each others' bodies.

When you get that stuck feeling, you can't bull your way out by hitting the problem over and over. Change tactics. After you have tried something six different ways, drop it and give it to your subconscious mind. Define criteria for a solution. Then forget about it. Leave the studio. Occupy yourself with a diversion: nap, walk, exercise, talk, eat. Trust your unconscious to untangle it for you.

Artists Who Create Too Much: Cutting

Usually by the time you know the shape your work needs to take, you will have accumulated too much material. It's time to get the scissors and shear stuff away. If you comb through your piece, ruthlessly cutting whatever hangs away from your shape and goal, you will sculpt a finer product than if you keep it all.

In TOUCH, some of our hardest arguments revolved around cutting. We each wanted to keep our favorite parts, and lobbied for them when the knife approached. When we butted heads, we referred to the statement of the piece. If a part didn't contribute to the statement, we axed it.

Brian Clark, author of *Group Theatre,* wrote that he goes through a new script word by word, asking, "Does this add anything significant, or is it just padding?"[2] We asked, "What does this say? How does it move the action forward?" If we kept getting the same answer, we cut.

Kill Your Babies

Some people develop such an attachment to their work that they can't cut it. They need a director, editor, or dramaturg if they want to avoid creating a mishmash and leaving their audience overstimulated, confused, and exhausted.

Davidson Lloyd of Keegan and Lloyd said:

> If you've got ten wonderful ideas and you really only need four, then you have to be strong enough to say, "OK: six of these ideas are going to die." They may appear in another piece. . . . After the audience has seen four, the audience doesn't care about the other six. You need that discipline to say, "OK, the piece ends here. It doesn't end here, here, here, here, and here. Let's not beat the audience to death with five endings."

Wait and See

Liz Lerman, artistic director of the Dance Exchange in Takoma Park, Maryland, mentioned that some editing decisions happen by letting the process take its natural course.

> It's not so much a reluctance on my part to make decisions. Sometimes artistic decisions get resolved on their own terms, if you wait long enough. . . . I don't have to step in and edit people's stories, because if they keep rehearsing, they'll edit on their own, either consciously or unconsciously.

The Creative Process in One Paragraph

The process of creating a performance piece can be summed up in one paragraph. To get started, do something to find an idea. Try any of the twenty-two methods in Chapter One. When an idea or image tugs at you, investigate it further. Open a file. Gather material. Try something, discuss it, decide on what you like, and ask questions to find the next step. Then try something else. Whenever you can, decide on a structure, sequence, form, genre, design in space and time, or build for the piece. Use the one-element-at-a-time creative process to deepen your work. When you get lost or stuck, change tacks, go back to your original idea, or work on one of the central elements to gain clarity. Use organizing tools like Post-it Notes or index cards scattered on the floor to envision the whole. Use one of the collaborative writing processes in this chapter to create a text. Finally, have the courage to cut when you create too much.

Have faith that, if you keep working on it, something marvelous will evolve over time. Invest the time it requires.

It Takes Time

In 1981, TOUCH spent eight, forty-hour weeks creating new material. We produced forty minutes of new work—five minutes of product per week—and we were speeding. By our seventeenth year, at our peak efficiency, we produced thirteen-and-a-half minutes of new material in a week. Keith Hennessy of Contraband in San Francisco talked about one "incredibly productive" four-hour rehearsal that brought up forty-five seconds of material.

Creating material takes so long because the process involves throwing out 99 percent of what you invent. You throw out piles of scintillating material, because it doesn't fit in the piece. A good deal of what happens in rehearsal has value only because it leads you to the stuff you never would have found if you hadn't gone that route. Enjoy the time it takes and the byways it takes you down.

When It's Over, It's Not Over

When you're finished composing, you're not finished. Many performers I spoke with said that performances are part of their writing process. They schedule rewriting sessions after opening performances. The audience teaches you things you would never discover in your studio. Each performance informs your process and prepares you for the next one.

Carlos Uriona, formerly of Diablomundo, a performance collective from Buenos Aires, and currently with Double Edge Theatre in western Massachusetts said, "For us the process never ends: we will change the work to match audience response. The audience completes the show like a circle which is open until the audience arrives."

Notes

1. Joseph Chaikin, *The Presence of the Actor* (New York: Theatre Communications Group, 1972), p. 28.

2. Brian Clark, *Group Theatre* (London: Pitman, 1971), p. 75.

COLLABORATIVE PROCESSES

Structuring Safety, Time, Power, and Decision Making

The second half of this book reveals practical things you can do to help your group work together better. This chapter explores the guidelines some groups use to keep the studio safe and productive, and then talks about ways to structure time and share power during rehearsals.

Why Have Guidelines?

Not every group can articulate their guidelines, but every group has some, whether they voice them or not. Unwritten rules cause discord. If no one has told everyone to arrive on time, and someone consistently shows up late, the on-time members resent the late one. The late one feels the resentment without understanding its cause. Resentment festers in a group that avoids confrontation, and can spoil the atmosphere.

Adam Gertsacov, clown, actor, and director, talked about *The One Sure Thing: A Cabaret on Death*, a performance he created collaboratively when he was a graduate student in Theatre and Communications at Rhode Island College. He used group psychology, group communication techniques, and leadership theory to structure rehearsals:

> All of the literature about group management and group psychology says that one of the very important things is to have ground rules. So the first day, we spent a lot of time agreeing to ground rules. For example, people should come on time. Agreeing to norms, normative behaviors: coming to rehearsal drunk was not acceptable. Some of these are obvious. Some were not so obvious.

How to Agree on Guidelines

The time to set guidelines is when your group first meets at the beginning of a project. (This is also the time to agree on issues of copyright, ownership of the work you will create, remuneration, and royalties.) Everybody affected by the guidelines should help craft them. Write each suggested guideline down so all can see. Include picky and obvious ones, like wearing appropriate clothing. Use positive language that describes observable behavior—rephrase the negative "Don't interrupt," to the positive, "Listen silently until each speaker finishes." Be specific: instead of "respect," delineate respectful behaviors, such as, "Listen open-mindedly," or, "Use affirmations." Clarify each guideline so that everybody understands it. When you finish the list, go through it item by item, until everyone agrees to try to abide by each one. If someone can't agree to one, leave it off the list.

Group agreements clarify your working process and eliminate secrets and hidden agendas. When everyone helps to compose them, everyone assumes responsibility for sticking to them, and everyone has a stake in enforcing them. You can change them as needs arise. Whenever someone new comes into the group, reconsider the guidelines together. Talk about the changes, and get agreement all around.

Creating Safety

Group agreements create safety. Creative groups need to nurture an atmosphere where people feel safe enough to take risks; otherwise, only heroes will bring forth creative ideas; others will censor themselves. Making art requires physical, emotional, and spiritual commitment as well as vulnerability and trust. Artists need to feel safe enough to move freely, experience feelings, and express themselves without fear of negative consequences. Everyone in a group holds the responsibility for maintaining a safe environment.

Here is a sampling of guidelines that I gathered from the groups I talked to. Some apply to specific types of groups; some contradict others. Like the elements of composition, you can choose guidelines that work for your group and the particular project.

Talk Safely

Steven Kent said that, as a freelance director, he spends time with each new group creating safety.

> I think it's probably the most important thing, to create a safe process. That does not mean a gooey, soft process. Things like the twelve-step program: "Leave it here. What's said here stays here." Another safe process is: you don't talk about other people if you can possibly help it. You may explore a problem with another person, but if you have something to say to a person, you say it *to* them, not *about* them. So people don't get paranoid.

Acknowledge Feelings

Feelings are facts of life. They are part of the working environment. We use our feelings to make our art. It is OK to have feelings and recognize them as they emerge.

Kent continued,

> Also saying to somebody, "Listen, it's getting hairy here," acknowledging fear, and talking about what feelings are in the room; . . . it's so strange to ignore people's feelings, when our whole profession is to generate emotions. You have to sometimes say, "That's enough. OK. You're afraid. We cannot handle the fear."

Separate Art from Therapy

If you use personal stories to create material, strong feelings will enter your rehearsal space. You will aid your process by developing sensitivity to boundaries, privacy, and the difference between art and therapy.

Martha Boesing, cofounder and director of the Minneapolis-based feminist collective At the Foot of the Mountain Theatre, talked about how boundaries sometimes got muddied.

You say, "We're not a therapy group," but it's hard to tell the difference sometimes. We were determined to tell the truth to each other, and determined that we would process everything. All interruptions were OK. That was one of the rules. Anything can be interrupted for what's going on with you. This is a safe space for you to say what's really going on with you. Well, what's going on with you might be that how much you hate your father has come up today. And you don't know that. And so what you're saying is, "I hate this person!" And you've referred it over and you don't even know you've done that. So if you don't have a lot of personal awareness . . . boundaries get very, very, very muddied.

Some artistic directors I interviewed stressed that part of their job was to make a safe environment and to monitor the feelings in rehearsal. A group therapy facilitator could say the same thing.

The difference between doing therapy and making art is that in therapy you try to contact your feelings and gain insight into their origins and connections in your own history. Therapy is about communicating with yourself: understanding the link between your past experiences and your present feelings and behaviors. In artmaking, you use those same feelings and behaviors to communicate to others. When you make art about personal issues, the dividing line between art and therapy narrows because your own history, and the emotions connected to it, become your subject.

Don't Share What Will Upset You

Groups that don't want to deal with personal issues erect boundaries between what belongs in the studio and what doesn't.

Adam Gertsacov wanted to use personal stories from his collaborators for his show, *The One Sure Thing*, but he didn't want them to get upset in rehearsal. When they were making guidelines, he clarified the boundary:

> Another rule . . . because we were dealing with a lot of personal issues, was not to bring in things that were going to make you cry, or things that you weren't comfortable sharing. I wasn't interested in being a therapist; I was interested in telling stories. I wanted them to make sure that they protected themselves. To be very clear: this was not about personal discovery, it was not about going through very harsh stuff in your past. What it was about was building a play.

Flag on the Play

In TOUCH, we had a process called "flag on the play" for times when rehearsal felt dangerous, the emotional climate got weird, or someone obstructed work by acting like a jerk. Like football referees, anyone could throw a figurative flag and stop rehearsal. We would come into a circle to discuss what was going on until everybody felt clear. Then we resumed rehearsal. Since we were less likely to act out if we knew someone could confront us about our behavior, having the option of tossing a flag actually reduced the need for it—we rarely resorted to it.

Acknowledge Biology

In TOUCH, acknowledging our biological needs and taking care of them—like maintaining adequate blood sugar levels—kept us sane and safe. We had a rule that whenever I was hungry, we would take a snack break. Jef wasn't allowed to eat sugar when he was working.

Make It OK to Fail

> "You've got to be willing to fail; to fall flat on your back and try again."
>
> —Tom Keegan, Keegan and Lloyd.

Few can repeatedly fall and rebound without encouragement. Don't make fun of each other for trying things that don't work. Putdowns, sarcasm, and teasing wilt creativity. Embrace failure as if it were your peculiar sister.

Don't Hurt Anyone

Christine Murdock, former actor/director with the Road Company in Johnson City, Tennessee, brings some of the company's agreements into the classroom when she teaches:

> When I do workshops, there'll be games: "Try to get the other person to listen to you, anything to get them to listen to you. You cannot hurt them. This is a safe space. You cannot hurt people. . . . That's physical and emotional. You can't be mean. Don't use theater games to be nasty to each other."

Try Everyone's Idea

Naomi Newman, of San Francisco–based A Traveling Jewish Theatre, said,

> The *only* way I think it can work is when all ideas are recognized and explored to some degree, and not vetoed before some kind of exploration is done. That's what we came to in A Traveling Jewish Theatre. It used to be that somebody would come in with an idea . . . and two people would say, "No, that won't work." . . . We finally realized that that was really not a good thing to do, either psychologically or creatively; that we would always give the idea some energy and some attempt to explore it before anybody said, "That won't work."

If You Don't Do the Work, Don't Criticize the Product

In TOUCH, if I were going to build a mask for a piece, we talked about its parameters before I started, and everyone could make suggestions about construction. Once I finished it, we didn't allow criticism of it, because I did all the work. If someone had serious problems with the mask, she could build another.

Leave Life's Baggage Outside

In TOUCH, to keep the rehearsal space physically and metaphysically clean, we agreed that when we arrived at the studio, as we took off our shoes, so we also would leave our problems, emotional upsets, and worries outside the door. I endorse this rule, but I can't always abide by it. I try to enter the workspace in an open and neutral state, but when I am grappling with serious issues, I can't always let go of them. It wasn't until Steven Kent introduced us to *check-ins* that I solved this dilemma.

Structuring Time in Rehearsal

Check-ins

Check-ins air out secrets and hidden agendas. If you just had a fight with your partner, you say so. Then everybody knows what's going on. They won't have to guess about your mood, wonder if they're responsible, and get angry at you for walking under a cloud.

Martha Boesing explained that At the Foot of the Mountain was the first theater company to use check-ins in rehearsals:

As feminists we had been part of all this rising up of support-group work that feminists were doing, and consciousness-raising work, and we realized that we were very out of touch with our own lives, with what we felt, with our own sense of being oppressed. . . . We did what we called the feeling circle, or check-in. . . . There are theaters, to this day, that do this, that got it from us.

We . . . did that [every day] religiously. And sometimes those would go on for two or three hours because we were such an intense family that we had to really work through and process things that were going on between us. We did it before every business meeting; we did it before every rehearsal. . . . You just go around the circle and say what you're feeling.

The Five Lesbian Brothers use a check-in whenever someone needs to talk about feelings, to keep emotional channels open. They might do a check-in once a week, or at the end of a rugged rehearsal day.

You can check in spiritually, mentally, emotionally, and/or physically. For example, "I'm feeling tired and cranky because I couldn't sleep last night." Or, "I'm feeling anxious about how much work and how little time we have." You can ask for what you need: "My shoulders hurt. I would love a short massage." Check-ins clear the air about conflicts: "I'm angry because yesterday you said X and it felt like a put-down."

News

In TOUCH, we started each day with small talk. I thought it was a waste of time until I realized that we were building ensemble while we chatted—we subliminally checked each other out, reforged connections, and got comfortable enough to proceed with the hard work of creation.

Warm Up

Most of the groups I spoke to warm up together. Barry Mines, former director of Lime Kiln Arts in Lexington, Virginia, said that their warm-up routine varies from play to play:

We start with a fifteen-minute warm-up, that's vocal warm-up and physical warm-up. . . . For me, my biggest justification is that you gather everyone in a circle and you get everyone focused on doing one thing, then you can move on to the next thing. It gives you the chance to drop any other outside baggage that you'd be carrying through the day. . . .

It's the collective ritual of doing something that gets everyone in the framework of working together. And I've found that when people do not participate, that the rehearsal process suffers. It takes a while to get off the ground, and it's much more haphazard.

In TOUCH, we took turns leading a daily warm-up. We included physical and mental gymnastics, trust building, vocal work, improvisations, and energy exercises to reestablish our connections. We also included any skill work or technique we needed to practice for current productions.

Toning

Keith Hennessy, of San Francisco's anarchist-inspired collective Contraband, talked about evolving their warm-up rituals:

> For a while we were trying to create a new form for the warming-up of interdisciplinary performers. It was based on . . . being simultaneously a meditation and a vocal warm-up and a physical warm-up. We would go through a whole series of postures, where the sounds were about aligning the chakra systems, but the movements were based on a modern dance floor-barre. We got very involved: it took over two years to make this form. . . . The toning has lasted the longest: stand in a circle, inhale, make one sound.

Lab Time

The Bloomsburg Theatre Ensemble schedules three or four hours every week for lab time, or research and development. Gerard Stropnicky said, "We can do anything we like—anything from [making puppets] to [studying] flamenco. . . . We bring in teachers to teach us things we don't know, or we do research ourselves."

Wednesday Meetings

Sue Schroeder, artistic director of CORE Performance Company in Atlanta, described their weekly meetings.

> We take one-half of one rehearsal a week, and it's not meant to be a bitch session, though it can be. It's meant to be either to discuss some aspect of the piece verbally at length, or anybody can bring anything to the table. . . . Just making it an OK place or a safe

place to have that kind of dialogue. So anything and everything comes up.

Rehearsal Evaluation

If you evaluate your rehearsal process each day, you will continually improve how you do what you do.

Djola Branner, who worked with San Francisco's trio, Pomo Afro Homos, said, "At the end of a rehearsal, often we would have some type of critique about the process. . . . We'd talk about what we had done that day, evaluate what worked and what didn't, talk about how we might proceed."

Homework

At the end of each TOUCH rehearsal, we assigned homework, such as "Learn this sequence" or "Bring in an ending for this scene." Homework can mean research, skill work, or prop gathering. Homework takes you to the next step. It generates solutions to your stumper question. It starts the next day running—people want to show their homework, so they are eager to get to work.

Check-Out

We ended rehearsal with a check-out: each person says how he feels. A check-out opens a window for airing problems that arise during the day. If the creative process has stalled, people express frustration. If a conflict has come up, a check-out may clarify or resolve it. By expressing how the day has affected me, I can leave my feelings behind as I leave the studio.

Affirmation Circle

Marlene Johnson, an Atlanta-based radical therapist,* talked about giving affirmations in a "stroke circle":

> Strokes are specific appreciation for yourself and the others in the circle. You give one for yourself, for something you are happy or proud about, and one for each person in the circle, specifically what you appreciate about what they did.

---

*Radical therapy combines feminist theory and group therapy techniques that developed in the '60s and early '70s in California.

Another option is to stand in the center of the circle while, one at a time, people tell you what you are doing well, where they see you growing, and in what specific ways they appreciate your contributions to the work.

Structuring Power in Rehearsal

Here I describe two power-sharing structures in some depth—rotating ogreship and consensus decision making—and then briefly sketch a few others, including collectives and variations on traditional directorships.

Rotating Ogreship: TOUCH

Rotating ogreship sounds silly; nonetheless it is a serious tool that allows a group to share power equitably, to encourage creative contributions from everyone, and to open up the decision-making process.

When C. W. Metcalf guest-directed TOUCH, he developed rotating ogreship to demystify, simplify, and equalize decision making. We used and modified the process for the rest of the life of the company.

Rotating ogreship means we take turns being an ogre. When it is my turn, I am the ogre; the others are my peons. We work on what I want to do; we try my ideas.

Ogres and Peons

When I am ogre, my peons try to please me. I tell them what element we are working on, what I want to try, and what each person's job is. Viola Spolin would call a job a "Point of Concentration."[1] I give each peon one job. He may ask clarifying questions, but he may not grumble about my idea.

After we finish trying my idea, I thank the peons. As ogre, I assume responsibility for failures and endow my peons with credit for success. Then I lead the discussion about the element we worked on, what worked, and what we can keep. We end with decisions. I can make unilateral decisions, or I can incorporate the opinions of my peons. We write down our decisions. We can change them later, but for now we have a place from which to take the next step.

When we finish working on my idea, after an hour or two, I give up my ogreship and pass it on. Now I become a peon, and I must please my new ogre. If, as peon, I have an idea to try, I may ask my ogre to entertain it. She can refuse to listen, or listen and choose to use it or not.

Super-Ogre

The super-ogre "owns" the concept. He came up with the original idea; he holds the vision. The super-ogre rotates between ogre and peon like the others, but he has the final say over his piece because he carries the clearest vision for it. Like Frodo, the Ring-bearer in J. R. R. Tolkien's *Lord of the Rings*, his companions can voice opinions and try ideas about where to go next, but they follow him, because he carries the burden of the Ring to its end.

The super-ogre cannot stop anyone from trying an idea for his piece. He must let his collaborators infiltrate his thinking and influence the work.

The beauty of collaboration springs from this very contamination of one person's idea with another's. People who didn't dream up the original idea perceive it differently, and try out tangents and skewed visions, which the originator might never imagine. Collaborative work has an originality that grows from this cross-pollination. The super-ogre must honor the collaboration by receiving his peons' contributions with an open mind.

As long as time permits, anyone can, as an ogre, work on anyone else's piece. After an ogre has tried an idea to his satisfaction, the super-ogre can accept or veto it.

Sub-Ogres

I can pass my turn on to a sub-ogre, who then runs my turn. When he finishes, I thank him and my ogreship is over. Sub-ogreships come in handy when one person has expertise. I can ask the musician to run a singing session. Sub-ogreships allow everyone to contribute their strengths to the group in a timely fashion.

Long-Term Ogres

Steven Kent recalled that when Provisional Theatre experienced difficulties with power sharing, they brought in a facilitator, Dr. Terry Kupers, to help them sort out the muddle.

> He did some group therapy on . . . Provisional and helped us out. . . . He talked about, "You guys are so collective you are

stymied." He said, "OK, you don't like hierarchy. But how about doing this: How about saying there are hierarch*ies*. For instance, . . . when something like the car falls apart don't you all go to the technical director? And when it comes time for leading singing, don't you go to the person with the best ear? And when it comes time for sitting outside and shaping things, don't you all go to Steve?" He said, "Well, accept them. There isn't *a* hierarchy . . . but you do have hierarch*ies*. And, let's name them." And that clarified us.

The person who best can load the van becomes long-term loading ogre and has final say over where things go. The best writer becomes long-term dramaturg; the best director, long-term director. Everyone can contribute to these arenas. A long-term ogre doesn't deprive anyone of creative contributions. He acknowledges and capitalizes on everyone's strengths.

Why It Works
With rotating ogreship we made steady progress; all our ideas got a chance on the boards; we could weigh everyone's opinions and make decisions; we kept dominant personalities in check, and we gave equal time to less assertive ones.

Before we began using it, we would tussle over moment-to-moment control of the group, and dicker over what to do next. With rotating ogreship, we just asked, "Whose turn is it now?" The next ogre quickly decided on a course of action, and his peons happily followed. We spent more time creating pieces, and less time dithering in decision-making limbo. We eventually appointed an ogre for every task, from painting props to giving an interview. Rotating ogreship made us more efficient creators and happier collaborators.

Rotating ogreship lets everyone know who's in charge. An ogre can handle disagreement over how to write a scene. He can try everybody's idea, combine ideas, choose his favorite—whatever he does, if his peons are unsatisfied, they can try their ideas when they get to be ogres. Rotating ogreship distributes responsibility for running rehearsals. Knowing that I will be ogre prods me to plan a next step.

Consensus Decision Making: Cornerstone Theater Company
David Reiffel worked as composer-in-residence with Cornerstone Theater Company for their first five years. He described how they first handled disagreement:

Meetings weren't run very well. It was basically anyone talked, and
. . . whoever talked loudest and jumped in first got the most said.
And somebody noticed.

It became clear that we were collaborating within a very strong
hierarchy that those of us who had fairly strong artistic personalities sometimes were running up against in really painful ways. . . .
People who were working within the collaboration wanted a better-
codified way of making the decision that included them in a powerful way. And that's when we hit upon the idea of consensus: a
strict vocabulary of consensus and consensus process.

Consensus refers to a rigorous decision-making model with a specific
vocabulary. "Eventually," Reiffel said,

> we used consensus in business meetings . . . figuring out the sched-
> ule, dealing with the fact that so-and-so up the road had objected
> to this material in the script, and was threatening to quit the
> show; basically, for everything that didn't fall under a person's ar-
> tistic purview.

Facilitator

Various members of consensus groups assume responsibility for running their meetings by taking on certain roles and tasks. Reiffel explained that the facilitator plays a crucial role.

> The facilitator is not allowed to speak for him- or herself without
> handing over the facilitation to someone else. . . . The responsibil-
> ities of the facilitator are: calling on people whose hands are up;
> keeping a list. You don't sit there with your hand up while some-
> one else is talking. You just signal the facilitator that you wish to
> speak, and the facilitator keeps a running list of who is speaking.
> It's a tough job. . . .
>
> The facilitator is the person who says, "I think we should split
> up into small groups. I think you two should go off and work this
> out," maybe sending another facilitator, a cofacilitator, along with
> them. . . .
>
> [The facilitator's job is] to try to guide to a consensus. To see
> what the sense of the meeting is. The facilitator can offer a clarifi-
> cation. It's not a position of imposing views, which is why the fa-
> cilitator is not allowed to speak to an issue without handing over
> the facilitation.

Decisions are made through mutual consent. The course of action is something that everyone can consent to, not that everyone loves, but that everyone can live with, basically.

The facilitator also

- balances people who talk a lot against quieter ones;
- elicits input from quiet ones;
- keeps the group on time and follows the agenda;
- clarifies muddy statements;
- identifies common threads;
- summarizes agreements and disagreements;
- makes sure all ideas are heard and understood; and
- tests for consensus, which means expressing what seems to be emerging from the group process.[2]

Timekeeper, Note Taker, and Role Rotation
Because the facilitator's tasks are complex, some groups break down the job and assign tasks to different members. Reiffel said that Cornerstone used

timekeepers—usually there was an agenda to which time allotments were given. And note takers—notes were kept in a notebook to which everyone had access. The other important thing was a rotation of facilitators and note takers. Note takers tended to facilitate the next meeting. We tried as much as possible to make sure that different people facilitated the meetings.

Gatekeeper, Empath, Devil's Advocate
The gatekeeper takes care of who will speak and in what order, thus freeing the facilitator for enabling, monitoring, and summarizing discussion. The empath monitors the emotional climate and suggests ways to deal with it. If the group gets bogged down, the empath might suggest a ten-minute break and lead a stretching and moving game. The empath names feelings that people express nonverbally and invites them to speak, thereby clearing the air.

The devil's advocate names the problems a proposed idea might engender. Envisioning the worst-case scenario is part of good planning. Rotating the devil's advocate role brings negative outcomes into the planning process without blaming anyone for mentioning them.

Vocabulary

David Reiffel also elaborated on some consensus vocabulary.

Concerns: "People can have a concern, which is one level of objection. And it has to be addressed. People's concerns have to be addressed before you can move forward with the action, which is the big thing that makes it difficult."

Blocking Concerns: "If you have a blocking concern, (you can still have a concern, but if it's not a blocking concern, the thing can still move forward) you can say, 'I want to block this action.' And then it has to be talked out. Either that blocking concern has to be addressed, or you have to find a second or a third or a fourth solution."

Standing Aside: "Standing aside is a formal way of saying, 'I don't agree with the action we're taking, but I realize that that's my [issue].' Or, 'I don't agree for reasons that have more to do with me than the actions of the company.' In more contentious issues, that happens a lot."

Round-Table: "A round-table [means] you go around to everyone to make sure that everyone can say something about the issue."

Modified Consensus: "We also used a modified consensus model, in that . . . ultimately, if the group could not come to consensus, the cofounders would make the decision, which sort of cuts off . . . having to find another solution."

A Consensus Decision-Making Flow Chart

A consensus decision-making process, looks like Figure 5–1 on p. 100.[3]

If the group fails to come to an agreement, four questions lead to the next step:

- Do you need more information?
- Do you need more time to think?
- Do you need more time to talk?
- Can those who disagree stand aside?

Consensus decision making works for groups who are willing to attend to the skills it requires—listening, attending to and validating

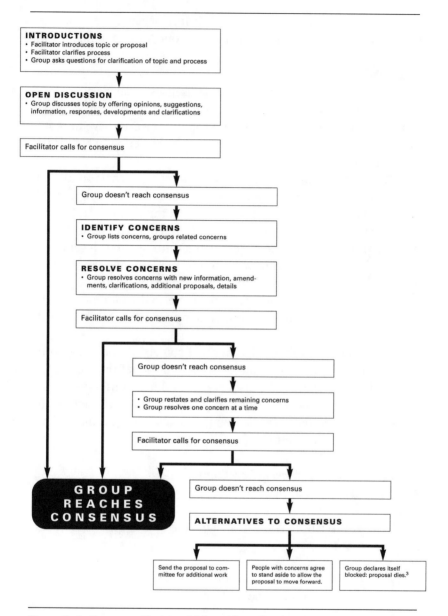

Figure 5–1. Consensus Decision-Making Flow Chart

emotions, creatively weaving varied points of view together, patiently working through conflict, and summarizing. My experience with consensus groups is that they take less time, reach better decisions, and leave members happier with each other and with their decisions than voting groups.

Other performing groups have developed different ways to share power and responsibility. Some are more collaborative than others, but each method adapts to the needs of the company.

Evolving Structures: San Francisco Mime Troupe

R. G. Davis founded the San Francisco Mime Troupe in the early 1960s. Davis collaborated with other artists to produce agitprop musical comedies.

At first, Davis incorporated the ideas of company members into the work, while retaining the final say over artistic decisions. Then, he established a self-appointed *gerontocracy,* in which the older members formed a committee of decision makers. Later, company members elected an *inner core*—a group of five who set company direction, instituted policies, and suggested salaries.[4]

Currently, the Troupe functions as a collective of artistic and production people. The administrative staff works for the collective. The Troupe casts roles by evaluating members' desire and ability, and by listening to members' discussion of the work in question. The actors help with administrative duties and technical work. The technical director also writes plays and manages tours, for example.

Dan Chumley, director and actor in the Troupe, described the process of deciding who does what as, "spin the bottle, or spin the finger." The group expects people with seniority to rotate in and out of different jobs. When something needs to happen, someone will say, "It's my turn to take this on," or someone else will point a finger and say, "Your turn."

Collectives

In some collectives, members live and work together and share their resources with the group. Some are actor-run, like the Company Theatre in Los Angeles. In the 1960s, Company Theatre actors rehearsed daily, and then did administrative and technical chores. Other collectives, like Julian Beck and Judith Malina's Living Theatre in New York of the 1960s, are director-driven. In some, everyone divvies up the theater's income equally. The feminist collective At the Foot of the Mountain paid everybody the same base pay, with additional stipends for the artistic director and manager, for women with children, and for people with longevity in the company. They charged a sliding scale for tickets.

Keith Hennessy talked about the San Francisco anarchist-inspired collective Contraband in the 1990s:

> Because we spend a lot of time together, we really try to see our collaborative process as community based: as a process by people who live and work together. And it's partly what makes us strong, I think. . . . We have a lot of interconnected personal lives. . . . We might do some of the same rituals or celebrations or other social activities together, but we all live very close to each other, and we've been rehearsing in the same studio for the last eight years . . . and some of the people in the company live in the building.

Modified Directorships

Many collaborative companies have an artistic director. The directors I spoke with placed their power structures along a continuum between the autocracy common in traditional theaters on one end and the formal anarchy of certain collectives on the other. A few companies come to mind: Goat Island in Chicago, El Teatro Campesino in California during its first fifteen years, and Liz Lerman Dance Exchange in Takoma Park, Maryland.

Choreographer: Liz Lerman Dance Exchange

Liz Lerman said one of her functions is to come up with movement phrases, questions, or problems which she poses to her dancers. When I interviewed her, she was preparing for rehearsals for a piece on the Underground Railroad. Realizing that the word *harbor* would have importance in the piece, she described a series of structures she might set up for her dancers to try around the word:

> I'd say, "Figure out how to hold somebody against a building. Hold it for what you think is thirty seconds, and then you can move again and connect, and hold them for what you think is thirty seconds."
>
> So we'd try that, and I would watch it. And as I'm watching it, I would discover what the problems were. And I would say to them

when they had finished, "What did you observe? What did you discover?" . . .

So I would imagine that they would say something like . . . "Well, I had no idea when thirty seconds was up. It got in my way having to count to thirty." So we would solve that: "Well, let's try it again, but hold it as long as you want to." Or I would imagine someone saying, . . . "I found a couple I really, really liked." And I might say, "OK, let's share the ones that we liked." And we would learn ten positions, and we'd do it again, just working on the ten positions. And we'd start refining it.

Then Lerman might ask them to improvise a sequence of holds against the wall and transitions in and out of the ones they learned. Lerman retains final say over the choreography, but her dancers create much of the material in response to her questions or improvisational structures.

Three Codirectors: Theatre de la Jeune Lune

When Minneapolis-based Theatre de la Jeune Lune began, according to Barbra Berlovitz Desbois, the three founding members codirected.

And that was interesting. . . . It worked pretty well because . . . we all direct very different aspects. One of us is very image oriented, and looks at the work in a very large sense. Myself, I tend to be very people oriented, actor oriented, so I wind up directing the actors a lot. The other person is very attuned to the architecture of the space, and directed a play in that direction. So it kind of worked that we all came from different directions on a piece.

When they disagree, Desbois said:

We ask a lot of questions. When we are up against problem solving, which, in many respects, that's what theater's all about, we talk about it. We talk about it constantly, and in all different ways.

We're very involved in all aspects of the production. We do not come into a production . . . and say, "OK, I'm directing. You're designing. You're acting," and each person has their job. There's overlaps all over the place. The company was created by actors . . . and it really has a philosophy that, no matter what anybody else does for a production, where it all comes down to the final line, the actor is the person in front of the audience, and the actor, therefore, should have a very large voice in what happens.

Rotating Artistic Director: Bloomsburg Theatre Ensemble

The Bloomsburg Theatre Ensemble in Pennsylvania elects an artistic director from within the group each year. The artistic director's job, according to Leigh Strimbeck, ensemble member, is that of a "powerless leader." She "listens to the collective and then speaks in its voice."[5] The actors in the core of the ensemble decide on each season's play list, using a consensus decision-making process. First they choose the plays they want to do, and then they elect a director for each one, from within or without the ensemble.

The ensemble director does not necessarily direct a lot of shows. When they bring in an outside director, the ensemble director acts as an outside eye, who helps solve problems. The outside eye may do joint problem solving with the guest director, or recast the show if an actor is failing. If the guest director strays way out of line, the outside eye can discuss problems with him, and, as a last resort, fire him. Gerard Stropnicky summed it up:

> It's very collaborative until the director is determined. Once the director is determined, it is hierarchical, with the fail-safe of the outside eye, which is like the artistic director, who listens to the actors.

Visionary Director: Junebug Productions

John O'Neal, founder of Junebug Productions in New Orleans, described a hierarchy where the person with the clearest vision of the work stands at the top of a pyramid of writers, director, actors, and technical crews.

> It needs to be understood whose vision gives shape to the initial effort. And I think in an artistic process, that is a crucial question, because the envisioning is of necessity subjective in nature. And it's going to rest on a lot of intangibles, and those intangibles may or may not be communicable to other people. The more far-seeing, the more profound, the deeper the vision, the less likely it is that it will be capable of tangible expression from the start. So I think it's important that people in the process honor that this is Sheila's vision, that we agree to help her to accomplish. . . . Always to have a

sense of where your north star is: I think this is a way of liberating the creative potential, rather than suppressing it.

Notes

1. Viola Spolin, *Improvisation for the Theater: A Handbook of Teaching and Directing Techniques* (Evanston, IL: Northwestern University Press, 1985), pp. 21–26.

2. This discussion on consensus comes from my conversation with David Reiffel, and Michel Avery, Brian Auvine, Barbara Streibel, Lonnie Weiss, *Building United Judgment: A Handbook for Consensus Decision Making* (Madison, WI: The Center for Conflict Resolution, 1981), pp. 51–57.

3. C. T. Lawrence Butler and Amy Rothstein, *On Conflict and Consensus* (Portland, ME: Food Not Bombs, 1991), p. 18.

4. R. G. Davis, *The San Francisco Mime Troupe: The First Ten Years,* with an introduction by Robert Scheer (Palo Alto, CA: Ramparts Press, 1975), pp. 98–99.

5. Todd London, "Gentle Revolutionaries," in *American Theatre* (July/ August 1991): 52.

Group Dynamics

What We Need in Groups, Ways We Get Power, Roles We Play, How Groups Behave

Understanding Groups

Understanding group dynamics—what we need from groups, how we get power, roles we play, and how groups behave—will help you understand your group. This chapter and the next give an overview of group dynamics from the fields of psychology, sociology, business communication, and peacemaking.

What We Need in Groups

When we join groups, we perform an intricate dance to get what we need. Research reveals that people in groups require three things:

- inclusion: belonging to a community
- affection: caring for others and being cared for
- control: both being in control and being controlled, including status and power relationships[1]

As individuals, we jockey to achieve a comfortable balance of control, inclusion, and affection in our relationships. Every group member, while attending to group tasks, is also adjusting levels of inclusion, affection, and control. Each member uses various ways people get power in order to find a comfortable balance.

Friction occurs when individuals have divergent needs. If one member is using the group as a substitute family, and another member desires minimal inclusion and affection in the group, they will clash. Group members do well to articulate how much they want from their group, and to accept varying levels of commitment to the group. One way to explore group members' needs is by playing games.

Let Me In! Let Me Out!

This game comes from group therapy.[2] All members of the group but one form a tight circle by holding each other by the shoulders or waist, or in some other manner. The excluded person does whatever she can to get into the circle. The others resist. If she gets in, she joins the circle. Then everyone discusses the experience.

Variation: All members but one form a tight circle, with the one person inside. She tries to escape. The others try to keep her in the circle. Discuss afterward.

Ways We Get Power in Groups

People gain power in groups through various means: articulateness, a track record, emotionality, charisma, knowledge, action, elections, promotions, appointments, and the ability to reward or punish.

When group therapist Dr. Terry Kupers consulted with Provisional Theatre, he talked about four of these avenues, director Steven Kent recalled.

> One is articulateness. The second is track record. Third is emotionality, and fourth is charisma. Power is defined as getting your way over other people. None of those things has to do with whether the person is right or not.
>
> Now if a person is articulate and emotionally forceful, they're going to win. . . . So you have to analyze: Where is this coming from? Is this coming from because this person has charisma, and that's all it is? . . . Why is power being gained in this group? And

does it mean that we should do this? We tend to think that the person who can articulate the problem well is right about the issue. Not necessarily!

Christine Murdock of the Road Company from Johnson City, Tennessee, described emotionality,

> Some people are persuasive because they're louder. . . . And some people manipulate through emotional blackmail. If I'm real loud, and I get real upset, and threaten to not like you as a human being if you don't do what I want to do, well, it changes the whole tone. As opposed to just calmly saying, "Sheila, do you think that's good, right there?" . . . That's not going to get as far as the big, emotional, loud, "I can't believe that! If you do that, I won't walk on the stage!"

Someone who has been a member of a group for a long time has a track record—she understands the group's history and mission and she has achieved success in certain areas—thus she gains power over newcomers. Knowledge is power, too. Part of the long-timer's power resides in her knowledge about the group. Some people (and government organizations) like to withhold important information from others, and thus gain power over them.

Another road to power is action. When Carlos Uriona founded Diablomundo, a theater collective based in Buenos Aires, the group members agreed that

> the people that handle the decisions are the ones that have the action. For instance, if we are developing a new project, and we agree that our project will be on X subject, the ones that start researching on that subject, that are writing, that start with movements, with visual images, those are the ones that finally would make the decisions. . . . The active people were the ones that were bringing in the oxygen to the organization, and they would have more power.

In hierarchical groups, people get power through formal status structures: they are elected, promoted, or appointed to a position with more power. Those who rise in the hierarchy gain the ability to reward or punish, and to hire or fire others.

A marine officer coined the phrase "passive-aggressive" to describe people with low status in an organization who gain power over their superiors by indirectly sabotaging a project while appearing to carry out orders. They forget, misinterpret, or lose orders, miss deadlines, botch jobs, have accidents, get lost, and use a host of other strategies while seemingly working hard and proclaiming good intentions. Passive aggression can wreak havoc on any group. Group members must honestly confront and vigorously oppose it.

Groups can play games that explore power roles and members' reactions to power. Here are two that are fun and quite useful.

Killer Monarch

Keith Johnstone invented this game to play with power.[3] The monarch, let's say a queen, begins on stage. A servant enters and tries to please the queen. The queen, whenever the servant does something she doesn't like, briefly explains how the servant has erred, and orders the servant to die. The servant dies a dramatic death. A new servant enters and tries to please the queen. When the new servant displeases her, she orders him to die. The servants try to live as long as they can. They try to avoid the mistakes of the corpses littering the stage. If servants are dying too fast, the queen can grant them each three mistakes before death.

Triangles

A game in which power moves from person to person is triangles. TOUCH developed triangles from an exercise used by Tony Montanaro. (When four people do it it's called squares, pentagons when five do it. Any number can play.)

In a trio, each person stands at the point of an equilateral triangle. They stand close enough that they can feel a connection, but out of reach of each other. They all begin facing in one direction, toward one point of the triangle, so that one person has her back to the other two, and the other two are side by side facing her. The person who can't see the others, in other words, the person with her back to them, begins as the leader. She moves according to her impulses, in such a way that the other two can move with her, exactly as she moves. If she locomotes across the floor, her two followers locomote with her, keeping the integrity of the triangle. When she turns to her right or her left, as soon as she can see the person on that side of her, she gives the leadership to that person. When she can see the new leader peripherally, and the new leader can see her, they share leadership and the triangle has only one follower. As soon as the new leader turns far enough that he cannot see the first leader, he becomes the sole leader.

Whenever a person in a triangle can see another person, he follows; whenever he can see no one, he leads. When a triangle is really cooking, the leadership passes from one to another often and without a glitch. It looks and feels like the movement itself is leading.

To achieve success in this game, each ensemble member concentrates on the other two. The group establishes and maintains an energy connection that is palpable. Each member surrenders to the movement. It leads the group; each person breathes in sync with her partners; leading and following merge.

Roles We Play

The individuals in a group come with a history. Adults tend to play the same roles in a work group that they played in their families as children.

The family whiner grows up to be a group's irritant personality; the family peacemaker mediates arguments. We react to stress in historical ways, too. If temper tantrums got results in family crises, they are likely to be used in a group crisis, too.

Some roles are inappropriate for the workplace—they don't get what we want, or they hurt others. Breaking the habit of dysfunctional behavior requires honesty, courage, and hard work. As At the Foot of the Mountain's Martha Boesing put it:

> I do think that therapy is important if you're from a troubled family, and who isn't? Most of us have had some kind of dysfunction in our background that we bring into our current relationships. . . . Through some kind of personal growth work—I don't mean it has to be therapy, it can be certain spiritual training, work with meditation—I think that each person individually needs to work on herself, so that she doesn't bring that work into the group.

Identifying the roles people play in groups may help you gain insight into the dynamics of your group. Most people use a small repertoire of behaviors. Figure out who in your group plays which roles.

Include yourself in your analysis. The most valuable information is about you. When you can identify your own tendencies, you can try other tacks when your natural inclinations don't work. You can't make anybody else change, but you can change your own behavior, becoming more flexible and effective.

Satir Archetypal States

Virginia Satir, a pioneering family therapist, found that people react to stress in a group by placating, blaming, computing, distracting, or leveling.[4] Each person uses one, two, or sometimes three responses. Satir named these responses "archetypal states."

The placater says, "Please forgive me. I am such a clumsy oaf." He agrees with others. His position is "I am helpless. I am worthless." He ingratiates, apologizes, and pleases to get his way.

The blamer uses fear and shame to control others. She shouts, "It's your fault, you clumsy oaf!" She looks down her nose, points at others, makes karate chops with her hand. The blamer disagrees. She's a faultfinder.

The computer's speech is impersonal. Instead of saying, "I'm so sorry; are you all right?" he says, "I wish to render an apology, I inadvertently struck you." The computer displays little affect. He observes, listens, evaluates, synthesizes, generalizes, and organizes. He speaks in a monotone. He gestures little—a lift of an eyebrow might be all you'll see.

The distracter diverts attention from anything serious. After he bumps into you, he says, "Gee some guy's mad. He must've gotten up on the wrong side of bed." He shifts his focus and body, bobbles his leg, chews gum. He ignores questions, changes the subject.

The leveler displays honest, congruent responses. Her feelings, body, voice, and meaning all match up. The leveler says, "I bumped you. I'm sorry. Are you hurt?" She changes her posture to fit the situation. Her movements are soft and flowing. The leveler is integrated, whole, alive, flowing.

Notice when you and others fall into these roles. Sometimes naming someone's behavior in a conflict and asking for an alternative will clarify a discussion. If you hear someone blaming, for example, you can say, "We aren't trying to decide who is at fault; we want to figure out what to do now." Or you can respond in kind, for instance, if someone speaks like a computer, you can answer like one, thus communicating on his level.

Each of these archetypal states can serve a purpose. If someone brings up a subject you don't want to discuss, distracting can change the subject. The states are dysfunctional when they are inappropriate to the situation; for example, if a distracter in a board meeting disrupts the meeting.

The Victim/Rescuer/Persecutor Triangle

One theory from Transactional Analysis states that two people can perform a complex dance around a triangle of roles: victim, rescuer, persecutor. They step from one role to the next as the dynamics between them change. Two people in an unhealthy relationship swap roles from moment to moment.[5]

Imagine a victim lying on the floor, calling for help. The rescuer runs to her and hoists her onto her feet. The victim embraces the rescuer, refusing to let go, even after she's been saved. The rescuer feels trapped and gets angry at the victim. He lashes out at her. Now the rescuer has shifted to persecutor. When the victim feels the anger of her former rescuer, now her persecutor, she gets angry at the persecutor, attacks him, and switches to persecutor. Thus she transforms her former rescuer/persecutor into her victim. The dance continues.

Radical psychiatrist Hogie Wyckoff defines a rescue as, "doing more for someone than she does for herself or doing something you do not want to do." Wyckoff says,

> It is impossible to save someone who believes she is powerless and unable to help herself. . . . Instead of being a compassionate and kind gesture, an attempt to Rescue someone is actually an oppressive and presumptuous act because it colludes with her apathy and sense of weakness. Rather than enabling women to take power and ask for what they want, Rescuing reinforces women's passivity and helplessness.[6]

Here are some other roles people play in groups:

- the silent one
- the peacemaker
- the quick thinker and the slow thinker
- the ambivalent one
- the expert
- the aggressor
- the repressed one
- the blocker

- the dominator
- the recognition seeker
- the self-confessor
- the playboy/playgirl
- the help seeker
- the special interest pleader
- the destroyer[7]

If you identify the roles people in your group are playing, you can get a feel for the basic dynamic tides tugging on your group. If someone takes on a role to the detriment of the group, naming the behavior may help things.

Group Behaviors

Groups have lives, just as people do. They are born, they flounder around looking for a purpose, they mature, they accomplish their life's work, they get old, and they die.

Groupthink
Irving Janis coined the word *groupthink*. He wrote:

> Powerful social pressures are brought to bear by the members of a cohesive group whenever a dissident begins to voice his objections to a group consensus. . . . [There are] group norms that bolster morale at the expense of critical thinking. One of the most common norms appears to be that of remaining loyal to the group by sticking with the policies to which the group has already committed itself, even when those policies are obviously working out badly and have unintended consequences that disturb the conscience of each member. This is one of the key characteristics of groupthink.[8]

Elephant in the Living Room
One symptom of groupthink is members colluding to avoid an issue. Twelve-step groups call the issue that people avoid the "elephant in the living room." In the case of a family with an alcoholic member,

the alcoholism is the elephant. When the elephant behaves destructively, family members clean up the mess without admitting they are cleaning anything up. Some elephants that appear in groups include

- lazy members, nonproducers, procrastinators;
- chronic latecomers, absentees;
- addicts, alcoholics;
- emotional bullies, mentally ill members;
- power cliques, gossips; and
- unsafe atmospheres due to lack of respect, sarcasm, criticism, cuts, ad hominem attacks.

Speaking your truth requires courage. Confrontation may feel scary. Nonetheless, the healthiest course is to name the elephant in the room, and unite to grapple with it.

Kill the Leader

Disgruntled members of a group play kill the leader. Kill-the-leader games include gossiping, backstabbing, sarcasm, jokes at the leader's expense, foot dragging, missing deadlines, subconsciously or intentionally misunderstanding or ignoring instructions, sabotaging projects, subconsciously or intentionally making mistakes that reflect badly on the leader, blaming the leader for the group's difficulties, and similar passive-aggressive ploys.

In collaborative groups, kill-the-leader games often result when the leadership goes unacknowledged. People act on hidden agendas to seize, undermine, or relinquish power.

Rita Mae Brown discussed leadership as it evolved in the Furies Collective, a feminist commune in Washington, D.C., which Brown cofounded in the early 1970s. She spoke of covert power centers and termed the one who really exerts power the *Hidden Task-Master* and the one who really holds the group together the *Hidden Maintenance Leader.*

> We spoke exhaustingly of equality. Only recently have we been able to discuss the underside of equality which is anti-leadership. . . . Anti-leadership plays into irresponsibility as well as national character. If you don't acknowledge leaders you aren't honest about your structure. Hidden leaders champion egalitarianism while de-

viously getting their way. If structure isn't made clear then ac-
countability isn't possible. . . .[9]

Scapegoating

The ancient Jews symbolically placed their sins on the head of a goat,
the scapegoat, and drove it into the desert as a part of the ritual
cleansing of Yom Kippur.

Scapegoating in groups targets low-status members. Groups that
shun responsibility for their actions assign blame to one member. In
a healthy group, each member assumes responsibility for his decisions
and actions, and accepts whatever credit—or discredit—they incur.

Groupthink, elephant in the living room, kill the leader, and scapegoating are dysfunctional behaviors. Here are some games that can
help eliminate dysfunctional group behaviors by heightening awareness of group leadership and teaching the ability to switch from
leader to follower.

Surge Game

Richard Schechner describes surge in *Actor Training 1:*[10]

> Everyone stand against a wall. On impulse one person moves to
> another wall, or large object in the room. Everyone follows, mov-
> ing in the same way as the first person (walking, running, crawl-
> ing, etc.). Everyone bunches up, breathes deeply, relaxes, spreads
> out. Someone else moves on impulse.

Surging encourages the group to see, accept, and instantly respond to one person's impulse, and to rotate leadership spontaneously.

First Variation: The mouse-in-the-house game. Ronlin Foreman,
who teaches at The Dell'Arte International School of Physical Theatre,
learned this from James Donlon. It begins with the group bunched
up in one corner of the room. They agree on a spot in the opposite
corner where a mouse sits. Without saying anything, they all watch
the mouse as it moves around the room, including up the walls and
across the ceiling, and they all stay as far away from it as they can
while always staying in a clump.

The mouse-in-the-house game clarifies the idea of group focus.
It requires kinesthetic awareness of the group.

Second Variation: A modern dance version of this game has the group moving continuously.[11] Whoever has an impulse to change the direction, dynamics, or type of movement takes the lead by changing it, and everyone else instantly changes to what he has started. This variation requires kinesthetic and visual awareness of everyone plus the agility to accept and instantly follow new impulses.

Being Together Game

In TOUCH, we invented a game called being together. Stand so that you can see the others. Each person focuses on the others, and responds to the slightest impulse with a complementary impulse. The improvisation can change radically or subtly at any moment, and everyone strives to stay together, to be there together, wherever *there* is, from moment to moment. You can use sound and movement, and mix literal and abstract impulses. One moment you might be marching in formation across a desert, the next careening off the walls of the studio and spinning and falling, and the next you might sit and pick nits off each other's backs like monkeys. The trick is to be together—in the same place, creating the same atmosphere, involved in the same activity—at all times.

Being together encourages openness to leadership from within and from others. It demands spontaneity, acceptance, and full-throttle commitment to the moment.

Group Cycles

Groups evolve over time. A new group displays different dynamics from an older one.

When I interviewed William Liles, who manages teams of computer designers for the Central Intelligence Agency, he explained how groups cycle through four behavioral stages over time: forming, storming, norming, and performing.

Forming

Forming includes orientation and ice-breaking behaviors. A newly formed group behaves politely; members show obedience and dependence; they respond tentatively to each other and make stabs at their task while they try to establish a common basis for functioning. They interact superficially. Their discussion lacks clarity while they build trust and foster cohesion.

Storming
During the storming phase, people state their opinions and disagree. People challenge each other's ideas, try to change each other's opinions, and vie for status. They resist their task. Opinions polarize the group; conflict characterizes the discussion; dramatic blowups occur.

Norming
After the storm comes norming. The group talks about its status and expresses the need to solve problems, resolve conflict, and complete its task. The group settles on norms for its behavior, and draws together into a cohesive unit. Acceptance, openness, and trust charge the atmosphere. Various members harmoniously share leadership, power, and responsibility.

Performing
Now comes the payoff: performing. Relationships stabilize. People align themselves toward group goals, and experience unity and cohesion. They comment favorably about the group, the task, and the members. They work creatively through conflict and discover innovative solutions to problems. The group gets results.[12]

Games to Strengthen Group Cohesion

Mirror Games
Mirror games foster rapport and intimacy, build inclusion and affection, and play with control.

Viola Spolin describes mirror games in *Improvisation for the Theater*.[13] The basic mirror game has two people facing each other: the leader moves and the follower mirrors her as closely as he can. Partners focus on each other. Here are a few variations.

Leaderless Mirror
The leaderless mirror works like the Ouija board: neither partner leads. They both concentrate on the other and follow the movement. It works if they pay attention to each other, if they follow the movement, if they don't try to think of what's next, and if they go with the flow. Leaderless mirrors teach people to trust in the movement, rather than initiating or directing an improvisation.

Instant Mirror

Instant mirror has a leader and a follower. The leader, at a cue like a drumbeat, suddenly explodes with a leap and freezes upon landing. The follower leaps and copies him instantly and precisely. After a while they switch roles. The instant mirror demands instant response to and acceptance of stimuli from a leader—a cornerstone of improvisation.

Oral Mirror

In an oral mirror the leader shoots words or numbers past the ear of the mirror. The mirror echoes instantly, shooting them back. The object is to reduce the time between the impulse and the response so that the two seem to speak simultaneously. Eventually, the leader tells a story one word at a time. The mirror tells it with him.[14]

Energy Catch Game

I learned this game from C. W. Metcalf. Energy catch hones several skills: focusing attention on a partner, movement observation, accepting impulses from others, and allowing a movement to evolve into something new—a form of creative thinking.

Two people face each other. Only one person moves at a time. The person who moves has a bundle of energy that causes part of his body to move a certain way—maybe his shoulder moves in circles or his spine shivers. With an obvious, direct thrust of the moving body part toward his partner, he tosses his bundle of energy to his partner who catches it exactly as he tossed it—if he tossed it hard and fast, her body recoils quickly from the impact. If he aimed at her head, her head takes up the same motion he threw her. After he tosses, he watches her in stillness. She lets his movement inhabit her, reproducing exactly what he sent her. She then lets it change in quality or migrate to a different part of her body before she tosses it back to him.

First Variation: Add more people. Keep the rule about only one person moving at a time.

Second variation: Two people move at a time. Toss a second movement into the circle, and keep both of them going. If one person receives two energy tosses at once, she accepts both, keeps them both going, changes them both, and tosses them both separately. The challenge to coordination can provoke giggles.

Third Variation: Add a sound to the movement; pass a sound and a movement simultaneously. Let the sound and the movement change concurrently.

Trust Games

When you perform with someone, you hold each other's lives in your hands. You trust your dance partner to catch you when you run and leap into his arms. Your acting partner trusts that you will play your part as rehearsed, or you might both "die" on stage.

You can build trust by playing trust games. They build a history of taking risks and practicing trustworthy behavior.[15]

It is important in the process of trust building to acknowledge and accept your own and others' feelings as they arise. Experiencing and disclosing feelings is part of the trust-building process. Sharing feelings is not mushy. It requires courage and calls out the best of us, our compassion. It fosters bonding. Leave time at the end of each game to talk about how it felt, when it felt scary, what someone said or did that helped, what memories it evoked. If someone needs reassurance or comfort, give it freely. If someone experiences fear and steps beyond it, affirm her courage. If you don't want to acknowledge and talk about feelings, don't play trust games.

Contact Improvisation

I learned this elementary contact improv exercise from Steve Paxton, dancer/choreographer, cofounder of the Judson Dance Theater and Grand Union, and one of the inventors of contact improvisation.

Stand with your weight on two feet. Close your eyes. Breathe and release any tension you don't need for standing. Pay attention to the small dance within you as your body maintains equilibrium, breathes, resists gravity. Feel how your bones support you and your muscles make myriad small adjustments to stay upright.

Partner up with someone close to you in size and weight. Gently touch your two foreheads together. Pay attention to the point of contact. By slowly rotating your heads, let the point of contact migrate. With your attention, follow the point of contact as it moves. Maintain one point of contact at all times. Think of the moving point of contact as describing an unbroken line wending along your bodies between you. Find a way to let the point of contact move from the head to the neck to the shoulder without breaking the line. Let the point of contact between you dictate where it wants to go next. Feel how your partner's weight affects you. Play with sometimes giving some of your weight to your partner. Respect your partner's limits.

This exercise introduces partners to touching one another, focuses attention on the point of touch, and experiments with weight exchange and balance. It asks each partner to follow the point of contact as it moves, rather than try to direct or control it. It builds trust between partners as they lean on and support each other responsibly.

Dead-on-a-Mat

In dead-on-a-mat, one person remains passive: he lies on a mat, face up. He closes his eyes and breathes, releasing tension, sinking into the mat like a dead weight. His partner gently picks up and moves one part of his body at a time. If she picks up an arm, she moves it to test for tension, gives it a gentle shake, moves the bones in their joints where they can go, lifts the arm, drops it, and catches it before it reaches the mat. He tries to give his arm entirely up to her. He does not help her with his muscles, and when she drops his arm, he lets it fall. If she feels tension, she helps him release it. She can say, "Give your shoulder to me." She can massage it. He can tell her if he feels uncomfortable or unsafe. She takes care to live up to his trust: she can not harm him, not even by a gentle poke. She can lift any part of his body that she can support safely.

When she finishes, they tell each other what they experienced. Then they switch roles.

Trust Circle

Trust circles crop up in group therapy, adventure teambuilding (Outward Bound, ropes courses), and performance class. Six or eight people create a circle shoulder to shoulder around one person. The center person stands with her feet together and her eyes closed, and leans in one direction. The people she leans toward reach out and support her upper body with their hands on her shoulders and upper chest. She keeps her feet still and her body straight as a board while the people supporting her pass her weight gently around the circle from neighbor to neighbor. Her upper body travels around the inside of the circle. Each person reaches out to support her as soon as she comes within reach, and continues to support her until she circles out of reach. If she can trust the small circle, the group steps back an inch.

In this chapter, we have seen some dynamics at work in a group: what people need in groups, ways people get power, roles people play, behaviors that groups exhibit, and games and exercises that foster ensemble. The next chapter explores functional behaviors—peaceful communication, group maintenance, positive critiques, and peaceful conflict resolution.

Notes

1. William Schutz, *The Interpersonal Underworld* (Palo Alto, CA: Science and Behavior Books, 1958), cited in Steven A. Beebe and John T. Masterson, *Communicating in Small Groups: Principles and Practices* (Glenview, IL: HarperCollins, 1989), p. 46.

2. Howard R. Lewis and Dr. Harold S. Streitfeld, *Growth Games: How to Tune in Yourself, Your Family, Your Friends,* with a foreword by Jane Howard (New York: Bantam Books, 1972), pp. 228–230.

3. Keith Johnstone, with an introduction by Irving Wardle, *Impro! Improvisation and the Theatre* (London and Boston: Faber and Faber, 1979), p. 71.

4. This discussion of archetypal states comes from Virginia Satir, *Peoplemaking* (Palo Alto, CA: Science and Behavior Books, 1972), pp. 49–50.

5. Hogie Wyckoff, *Solving Women's Problems Through Awareness, Action and Contact* (New York: Grove Press, 1977), pp. 90–92.

6. Ibid., p. 92.

7. Steven A. Beebe and John T. Masterson, *Communicating in Small Groups: Principles and Practices* (Glenview, IL: HarperCollins, 1989), pp. 65–66.

8. Irving L. Janis, "Groupthink," *Psychology Today* 5 (November 1971), 43.

9. Rita Mae Brown, *A Plain Brown Rapper,* illustrated by Sue Sellars (Oakland, CA: Diana Press, 1976), pp. 208–209.

10. Richard P. Brown, ed., *Actor Training 1* (New York: Institute for Research in Acting with Drama Book Specialists, 1972), p. 40.

11. Joyce Morgenroth, *Dance Improvisations* (Pittsburgh, PA: University of Pittsburgh Press, 1987), p. 20.

12. For the discussion of the forming-performing cycle, I am indebted to Tuckman, cited in Beebe and Masterson, p. 165.

13. Viola Spolin, *Improvisation for the Theater: A Handbook of Teaching and Directing Techniques* (Evanston, IL: Northwestern University Press, 1985), pp. 60–62, 66, 75–76, 175, 234–235.

14. Instant mirrors and oral mirrors come from Richard P. Brown, p. 117.

15. For more trust exercises, see Richard Brown; Satir, *Peoplemaking;* and Wyckoff, *Solving Women's Problems.*

Communicating Well in Groups

Peaceful Communication, Constructive Critiques, Conflict Resolution

Now that we understand something of group dynamics, we can deal with the two prickliest parts of collaboration: communication and conflict. This chapter explores three aspects of communication—peaceful communication, group maintenance communication, and constructive critiques—and looks at strategies for conflict resolution.

Reading about communication is easy, but don't be fooled. Just as understanding the mechanics of pirouettes does not mean you can do them, knowing about I-statements doesn't mean you can use them under stress. Improving your communication skills takes conscious practice over time.

Peaceful Communication

Peaceful communication does not mean wimpiness, any more than Ghandi's nonviolence weakened India's struggle for independence. Struggle and vigorous assertion comprise peaceful communication.

Peaceful communication comes from the thinking of the Religious Society of Friends, Mahatma Ghandi, Dr. Martin Luther King Jr., Native American councils, Eric Berne, and radical therapists.

Peaceful communication assumes we all have valid reasons for our thoughts, feelings, and behaviors. Far from taking an I'm-right-and-you're-wrong position, it requires the imagination to see an issue from someone else's point of view, and the empathy to accept someone's feelings as facts.

Peaceful communication involves wholehearted Active Listening, which means the listener reflects to the speaker what he is hearing, understanding, and feeling. Peaceful communicators use *I*-statements instead of *you*-statements. I-statements frame a problem so that the speaker assumes responsibility for his own needs and feelings.

Two parties in a peacefully conducted dispute invent a creative and fair solution together, so that both feel good about the results. They give affirmations and don't use put-downs.

Peaceful Communication Guidelines

The Religious Society of Friends has developed peaceful communication guidelines for consensus groups that would benefit any group. Consensus group members must commit

- to discuss in the spirit of consensus: a calm, friendly gathering to determine truth
- to suspend judgment if a session becomes unfriendly, or no decision comes out
- to listen to everyone; consider others' points of view
- to use silence as a creative tool; wait in silence when discussion becomes tense or repeats
- to take no action until all members are resolved
- to be willing to repeat this process patiently, as often as it takes
- to allow all key people to participate in the process
- to allow at the table only those affected by the discussion
- to allow everyone in the room to be heard
- to not interrupt
- to be willing to take into account who is speaking in order to evaluate what he says
- to be willing to separate power struggles from issues[1]

The last three guidelines—not interrupting, taking the speaker into account in evaluating what he says, and separating power struggles from issues—need some elaboration.

Talking Stick, Traveling Chair

Shelley Wallace, of Jest in Time Theatre in Nova Scotia, revealed that when company members get excited in a discussion, they use a talking stick to slow down. The talking stick comes from Native American councils. Whoever is talking holds the stick, like a low-tech microphone. When she finishes, she passes the stick to the next speaker. No one speaks without holding the stick.

The Society of Friends sometimes uses a traveling chair: when each person finishes speaking, she calls on the next person to speak.[2] Twelve-step group members signal when they finish speaking by saying, "Thank you."

Balancing the Speaker and the Speech

Taking into account who is speaking to evaluate the speaker's content involves balancing his experience, his communication skills, and his wisdom with his idea.[3] Some Friends meetings appoint a clerk who formulates the sense of the meeting by weighing what a person says against who says it. The clerk might assign less weight to an opinion from a new Friend than from an older Friend, for example.

Consider who speaks and how he speaks together with his argument. Then consider who speaks and how he speaks separately from his argument. The amount of power someone has in a group can blind people to the strength or weakness of his idea. A charismatic and articulate speaker can sway people toward a poor idea, while an unattractive and low-status speaker may have the best idea, but may not have the power to sway a group. Balancing the speaker and his speech means both taking into account who speaks to evaluate his idea, and evaluating the idea apart from who speaks it.

Strong Feelings

In TOUCH we gave more weight to someone with strong feelings for an idea than to someone with tepid feelings. If two people expressed mild reservations and one person spoke passionately for an idea, the passionate person moved the group in her favor, and would then carry the idea forward.

Power Struggles

Naomi Newman of San Francisco's A Traveling Jewish Theatre said we need to separate power struggles from issues:

> Sometimes [conflict] comes from a basic power struggle—"It's mine. I want it." . . . You're identified with wanting to have the power to do what you want to do. And every person who does collaboration has to recognize that truth about themselves: . . . there are times when it is just a downright power struggle. And when you know that, and can feel it, that's when you've got to take a break and let it go, and come back to it later. It's not going to be solved on the power struggle—"I'm right. You're wrong"—level. That's not collaboration.

Power Plays

Radical psychiatrist Hogie Wyckoff defines power plays as attempts to coerce someone so you get what you want. People use power plays when they feel scared or hurt. A childhood power play goes, "I'll be your friend if you do X." Some others:

- name calling: "You jerk"
- you-are statements: "You are so self-centered."
- threats: "I'll hate you. I'll quit. I'll get you."
- aggressive or hostile body language: raising the voice, pointing, frowning, sulking, slamming doors
- bursting into tears[4]

Listening to Self-Talk

Careful listening forms the bedrock of peaceful communication. Listening begins with listening to myself.

Self-awareness is the foundation of good listening. The way I listen depends on what I hear and feel within, as much as on what I hear and perceive without. To learn peaceful communication, I must examine my internal dialogue, or self-talk. If I put myself down, I will put others down. If I don't affirm myself, I won't affirm others. If I discount my feelings, I will dismiss those of others.

Recording my self-talk on paper or tape quickly reveals its quality. If I call myself "dummy, stupid, or nitwit," if I berate and belittle myself, then I am low in self-esteem. Negative self-talk sabotages my ability to work with others.

Changing Self-Talk

Changing self-talk takes daily, conscious effort over time. I must uncover the sources for my negative self-talk. I internalized the spoken and unspoken messages my caretakers and peers gave me as a child. I need to identify those voices I hear within and work to change the tapes.

Affirmations gradually overwrite our negative messages. An affirmation is a specific positive message—spoken aloud, spoken silently, written, or posted. Each person chooses affirmations that ring true for him or her:

- I am OK. I am safe. I will keep myself safe.
- I am lovable. I am loving.
- I am beautiful.
- I am creative. I have the resources I need within me.
- I am intelligent.
- I am strong. I am powerful.
- I am compassionate.
- I am a child of God, or of the Goddess. I am in God's hands. The energy of the universe flows through me.
- I am whole. I have everything I need.

Some people write affirmations down and post them on their mirror or their calendar. Some give specific affirmations for day-to-day struggles: "I showed patience and perseverance working on this problem." Or, "I acted courageously when I confronted so-and-so."

I can also affirm my ability to deal with a current challenge. "I can learn all my lines by the fifteenth and remember them effortlessly." Or, "I have the resources I need to accomplish X." Affirmations do not have to feel true. I might feel ugly, but if I tell myself I am beautiful often enough, I will begin to feel beautiful. The goal of repeating affirmations to myself is to achieve a respectful, loving, peaceful relationship with myself so that I can establish respectful, loving, peaceful relationships with others.

Active Listening

Once I start reframing my self-talk, I can reframe my communication with others. Dr. Thomas Gordon outlines a practical technique for effective listening, called Active Listening, in his book, *Leader Effectiveness Training*.[5]

Active Listening relies on two premises. First, when someone has a problem, he needs to be heard. Second, each person has within him the resources to solve his problems. Active Listening "shifts the onus of solving the problem onto the speaker,"[6] allowing the speaker to tap into his resources. It discourages rescues. The following example shows how Active Listening works.

Let's say Jim has a problem. If you think so too, you might start with door-opener questions or statements to begin a dialogue.

- Can I help?
- Would you like to talk about it?
- I'm interested in how you feel.
- What's on your mind?
- Tell me about it. Talk to me. Let's talk. Can we talk?[7]

If he talks, listen. Listen to the words, their meaning, his tone of voice, rhythm, speech pattern. Look at him. Watch the expressions on his face, his gestures, breath, and posture. Key into his energy and emotions.

If you listen fully, focusing all your senses on him, you will be too busy to formulate a response, argue, or do any other communication turnoffs. This is especially useful when his problem involves you.

While you listen, let him know he has your attention. Nod your head. Make listening sounds: "Mm hmm. Yeah." Physically show your interest: Tilt your head or lean toward him. Let your face express your concern and empathy. Give him the nonverbal messages: I hear you. I understand you. I accept you. When Jim pauses, you can respond in several ways:

- by reflecting content
- by summarizing and paraphrasing
- by reflecting feelings
- by encouraging
- by asking open-ended questions
- by asking clarifying questions

Reflecting Content

Reflecting content lets you check your understanding of Jim's story while telling him you're listening carefully. It sounds like this: "So, if I hear you correctly, Mary asked for your help; you dropped what you were doing to help her, and now you are behind schedule with the props."

Summarizing and Paraphrasing

Summarize his content when he has gone on for a while. "Let me see if I understand. Mary is taking more of your time than you have to give." Paraphrase what he says, using his vocabulary so he hears himself reflected. Or use your own vocabulary: paraphrase his inflammatory speech into neutral language. He says, "She comes barging in on me, bossing me around and demanding my help." You paraphrase: "She interrupts your work, and her manner is grating."

Reflecting Feelings

Reflect his feelings to validate his emotional experience. "You're upset about this. Mary's demands make you mad, and you're frustrated that you haven't finished the props." Express empathy, "I'd feel frustrated, too, if I were in your shoes."

Encouraging

If Jim has trouble articulating his problem, offer encouragement, either nonverbally—by nodding your head, making listening noises, or waiting silently—or verbally:

- Go on. I'm listening.
- Can you tell me more?
- It's OK to be upset. Take a breath and continue when you're ready.
- This is hard to talk about. Take your time.

Asking Open-Ended Questions

You can also lead him on with open-ended questions:

- And then?
- How did that go?
- Could you tell me more about this?
- What then?

Asking Clarifying Questions

Often people assume they understand when in fact they don't. In Active Listening, understanding is paramount. Jim might leave out information, or tell his story in a confusing way. If you don't understand, ask clarifying questions:

- Do you mean that . . . ?
- Are you saying . . . ?
- Do I understand you; Mary told you to forget about props?
- When you say "inappropriate," what do you mean?
- I'm not sure I get it. Can you say that in another way?

Defining the Problem

When Jim finishes, summarize the problem as you understand it. Include content and feeling. Ask him if you have gotten it right. Your summary, the problem statement, will help Jim work on solutions, so it is important that you get it right in his estimation.

"The problem is: If you don't devote your time to prop building you won't finish on time; Mary's demanding your time on the set, but you can't help her. You are getting frustrated as the deadline approaches. Is that it?"

Jim may amend it, add to it, or accept it. Or he may realize that he hasn't even gotten to the real problem behind the problem he has presented. "It's not that I can't finish my props on time; I can get volunteers to help. It's that I'm furious at the way she has been treating me, I can't stand working with her!"

At this point, you may want to offer helpful advice. But Active Listening does *not* mean giving advice.

Sometimes hearing the problem summary will lead Jim to a solution. "I need to tell her I can't help her for the next two weeks. After that, I'll be glad to help her." Or, "I'd like you to talk to her about where to go when she needs help. Tell her she's not my boss."

If Jim doesn't glom onto a solution once you've defined the problem, continue Actively Listening. Good questions to ask now are: So what do you need? What will solve this problem for you? What does a solution look like to you? Do you want to brainstorm some possible fixes?

Roadblocks to Listening

Many things that happen in ordinary conversation and seem inno-cent actually throw up roadblocks to problem solving. They stop the flow of talking and thinking which can lead to a solution. Some road-blocks to listening are[8]

- ordering, directing, or commanding, "You must . . . "
- warning, admonishing, or threatening: "You'd better . . ."
- moralizing, preaching, or imploring, "You ought, you should . . ."
- advising or suggesting solutions: "Why don't you . . . ?"
- persuading with logic, lecturing, or arguing, "The correct way to behave is . . . "
- judging, criticizing, disagreeing, or blaming: "You shouldn't have."
- praising, agreeing, evaluating positively, buttering-up: "You're so smart."
- name calling, ridiculing, or shaming: "You dolt!"
- interpreting, analyzing, or diagnosing: "You're really transfer-ring your anger with your mother."
- reassuring, sympathizing, or consoling: "Don't worry."
- probing, questioning, or interrogating: "Why did you?"
- distracting, diverting, minimizing, or kidding: "So what's the big deal? Let me tell you what happened to me."

Games to Build Listening and Reflecting Skills

Total Listening

By listening we express support and understanding. Good listening creates bonding. Miami-based performer and corporate trainer Darby Hayes outlined this Active Listening game.

Two people, Tom and Sarah, face each other. Tom talks to Sarah for four minutes about some topic—a favorite movie, something on his mind. For the first two minutes, Sarah does not listen—she ac-tively ignores Tom. After two minutes, she listens totally, with all her senses focused on him, maintaining eye contact. She does not reply; she only listens. When the time's up, they switch roles and repeat the exercise. Then they stop and discuss the experience.

This game demonstrates how rarely we experience quiet, focused listening. Listeners often mention how awkward it feels not to jump in with responses. We need to practice listening fully, because most of us rarely do it.

First Variation: The listener pays attention to the speaker's body language (or any other ingredient of communication). After two minutes she reflects his body language by imitating his posture, gestures, facial expressions, energy, and emotion. They discuss the experience and then switch roles.

Second Variation: The listener focuses on content and summarizes. The speaker can correct or add missing points.

Repetition Games
Sanford Meisner, a New York acting teacher, uses repetition games to train actors in the art of listening and responding honestly on stage. I cannot adequately describe the use or import of Meisner's repetition games here. They provide sharp tools for actors, and I recommend studying his technique.[9]

Listen and Respond Around
We used to play this game in TOUCH. Three or more people make a circle. Mimi makes a brief movement and pauses. The instant Jim sees it, he answers with a movement in response. The instant Joan sees Jim's response, she answers that with a movement. Then Mimi responds instantly to Joan's movement. It keeps going around. The movements can range from subtle facial twitches to full-body explosions. Focus on seeing the movement with whole-body attentiveness, and responding instantly.

First Variation: Add a sound to the movement.

Second Variation: Use sounds without movement.

Third Variation: Qualify the response; for example, the response must be an opposite of the initial movement.

Toning the Chord
Joseph Chaikin taught toning the chord to the Living Theatre, who performed it in *Mysteries.* The Open Theatre used it in rehearsals.[10] In one version, the group stands in a circle with their arms around each other. They breathe and listen intently to the breathing of their

neighbors. Whatever sounds each person hears, he responds with a similar sound of infinitesimally increased volume and intensity. The sounds the group makes depend on what each one hears, so they may build a chorus of giggles or wheezes or sustained tones. The sound builds to a peak and fades out at its own pace.

Seeing Duet
Family therapist Virginia Satir uses this game: Face your partner at handshake distance. Look at him for two minutes. Periodically close your eyes and picture him in your mind. Look at details—colors and textures, eyes and hair, wrinkles, bone structure, small movements. Meanwhile, your partner looks at you in the same fashion. To avoid self-consciousness focus all your attention on him. When the two minutes elapse, tell each other what you saw.[11]

True Mirror
Daniel Nagrin describes the true mirror.[12] Face your partner at handshake distance. Initiate nothing. See your partner and become your partner. Move only if your partner moves. Let your face and body become your partner's, your breath her breath, your impulses hers, your energy and feelings hers. Meanwhile your partner becomes you.

Group Maintenance Communication

Collaborative groups work better when everyone assumes responsibility for group maintenance. If everyone understands what the group needs to run smoothly, then everyone can pitch in to provide it.

Group-Building and Group-Maintenance Tasks
Steven Beebe and John Masterson, in *Communicating in Small Groups,* delineate the roles, tasks, and responsibilities vital for group maintenance:[13]

- encouraging members: "Thank you. I appreciate your saying that."
- harmonizing: "I hear Marquetta's idea as an extension of Jerome's. I can go along with it."
- compromising: "I'll give up X if I get Y."

- gatekeeping: "OK, Lynn, Bill, you've covered your idea pretty extensively. Let's give Sherry and Mike a chance to tell us their thoughts."
- setting standards: "Let's agree not to criticize ideas during the brainstorm."
- observing the group: "Everyone has spoken on this issue; it seems that the consensus is X."
- watching the process: "We have spent fifteen minutes gathering information, and another fifteen discussing options. Who is ready to decide?"
- monitoring feelings: "Some of us are getting punchy; let's break for lunch."
- initiating, contributing: "I have an idea."
- seeking information: "What happened about this last year?"
- seeking opinions: "What do you think?"
- giving information: "We used to do that; we stopped because X."
- giving opinions: "I think . . . , I feel . . . "
- elaborating: "What I mean is, Z."
- coordinating, organizing: "We need someone to write this proposal and get it to the printer by Wednesday."
- orienting: "We need to discuss this because, A. What we need to decide is, B."
- evaluating, criticizing: "I think the set design will work here, but it's too big to transport."
- energizing: "Let's take ten minutes to stretch."
- following procedures: "We agreed to vote after thirty minutes of discussion, and thirty minutes have elapsed."
- recording, taking notes

Responsibility for Individual Behavior

Everyone in a group needs to take responsibility for his own behavior. Those who tend to dominate discussion need to wait for others to speak. Those who seldom speak must volunteer their thoughts.

All need to acknowledge their own feelings and accept others'. All need to listen openly to others and seriously consider their ideas. Experts need to listen to nonexperts. All need to respect the ways of others.

All need to respond honestly to the group. All must try to follow group guidelines. All should spend more time listening than talking.

All must try to stay on task. All need to limit discussion to ideas and feelings, not personalities. Everyone must try to express thoughts concisely, and only once. Finally, all need to maintain a positive attitude, and use positive speech.

Defensive and Supportive Communication

To enable creative thinking and risk taking, group members need to engage in supportive communication, and avoid defensive communication.

Beebe and Masterson list supportive and defensive communication: [14]

Defensive Communication	Supportive Communication
Evaluate, criticize, use "you."	Describe, question, use "I."
Control or manipulate others.	Stick to issues; work for mutual satisfaction.
Display superiority, use put-downs, show off.	Express equality, mutual trust, and respect.
Express certainty, know all answers, take sides.	Admit "I'm wrong," display provisionalism, flexibility, openness.
Disconfirming Responses	**Confirming Responses**
Discount, deny.	Support.
Remain impervious, don't acknowledge others.	Acknowledge others and what they've said directly.
Respond with irrelevancies.	Agree about content.
Respond with interruptions.	Reassure, understand, sympathize.
Make fun of others' ideas.	Give clarifying response, ask questions, name feelings, encourage talk, paraphrase.
Respond with tangents: "Yes, but . . . "	Express positive feeling, "I'm glad you said that. I get it."
Respond impersonally: use "you, one, it, they."	Respond personally: use "I."
Respond incoherently.	Respond thoughtfully.

Games to Build Supportiveness Skills

Synectics—a system for enhancing group creativity—was developed to train teams of inventors. Synectics research has found that an "attitude of assistance" (or supportiveness) is a trait of creative thinkers.[15] The following exercises build an attitude of assistance.

Blind Offers

Keith Johnstone describes games based on "blind offers," which happen whenever one player offers an unidentified object or action to her partner.[16] The player thrusts her open hand at her partner and says, "Here, take this." An experienced improviser will take it, decide what it is, and use it in the improvisation.

In the elementary blind offer duet, the initiator takes a pose or makes a gesture, and the acceptor quickly uses the initiator in some way. Then the acceptor says, "Thank you," and the initiator goes away. For example, if the initiator makes claw-shaped hands, the acceptor can scratch her back on them. If the initiator bends over, the acceptor can sit on him, ride him, drive him, or write on him.

I Am a Refrigerator

My partner in TOUCH, Jef, adapted blind offers for young people. The I-am-a-refrigerator game teaches young people to develop supportive behaviors. Two members team up and take turns. When it is your turn, say, "I am a _____ ," and fill in the blank with an inanimate object. You take the shape of the object with your body. Your partner uses you as that object. When your partner finishes, he says, "Thank you." Then he says, "I am a _____ ," and takes the shape of a new object. You use him.

Children giggle as they sit on, write with, wear, and use each other. You can combine several related objects to create an environment that people move through. Meanwhile, children learn to make creative choices, touch each other without hurting each other, take turns leading and following, and work together to make a miniscene.

I've Fallen, and I Can't Get up!

Children in classrooms often hesitate to help each other. If someone gets into trouble in an improvisation, others would rather see him "die" on stage than rescue him. I invented this game for a small group, to get children used to jumping into improvisations to help each other out.

Evan starts an activity and develops a problem; Brooke enters and helps Evan by solving the problem; Evan says "Thank you" and exits; Brooke starts a new activity, and encounters a new problem. Robb enters, and solves the problem. Each initiator has three tasks: to communicate a problem, to accept whatever help comes in, and to thank the solver. Each solver enters as soon as he recognizes the problem, and solves it however he can. A simple problem, like falling down, can generate a simple solution, like a bandage, or a complex one, like an ambulance trip followed by an operation.

Evaluation

If you structure time for evaluation into all your group's activities, you will improve the way your group functions. To evaluate an activity, you must all agree on your group's goals. If you know your target, you can see how close you are to it.

Discuss what constitutes an excellent rehearsal, meeting, or residency to guide your evaluations. Marion O'Malley, director of the Center for Peace Education in Carrboro, North Carolina, asks these questions to find out what is working:[17]

What was effective?

What worked for you? What made it work? What was right for you?

What did you like that so-and-so said or did?

What helped and how?

To find out how to improve, she asks

What could have made it even more effective?

What could have made it work better?

What could so-and-so have said or done to make it more successful?

Note that these questions call for no negative language.

Peer Evaluations

Just as evaluation of each day's activity helps your group improve, regular peer evaluations help the individuals in a group improve.

The Committee on Nonviolence and Children of the Philadelphia Society of Friends[18] uses a cooperative evaluative process in which two people evaluate the work of one of them. They both write down as many positive things about the evaluatee's work as are true for them, then share their lists. Next, the evaluatee writes down the areas he needs to improve on and discusses them with the evaluator. Then, the evaluator adds any other areas for improvement. Then the two together prioritize the improvements and set goals and strategies to achieve them.

The Bloomsburg Theatre Ensemble uses a peer evaluation process at the end of each year. Each actor writes a confidential evaluation of every other actor's work and delivers it to him.

Constructive Critiques

People confuse evaluation and critique; it is important to understand the difference. *Evaluation* talks about processes, methods, tools, abilities, what is learned, and what is valuable—all in terms of agreed-upon goals. An evaluation places the activity and behavior on a continuum from high to low—from success to failure. A *critique* concerns the subjective, complex criteria that comprise a work of art. A critique doesn't deal with process; it deals with performance. Critiques take place constantly during rehearsals and after performances.

Agreeing on the Need for Criticism

D. Scott Glasser, a founding member and director of the Dakota Theatre Caravan, said that when they performed one show in repertory for several seasons, they

> shared notes after every performance of every show, for no matter how many years we did it. . . . Everyone contributed. A lot of it was in the form of questions. . . . We weren't damning. Understanding how stressful it could be, we discussed the issues around giving notes. The aim was mainly to keep it coordinated, keep the performing edge up, keep it clean, maybe come up with other ideas: keep it fresh. But it wasn't a matter of right or wrong. . . . Everyone agreeing and understanding that notes were a necessity [is what kept the play alive].

Looking for What Works

When C. W. Metcalf taught college, he said, he would ask for a critique of a piece, and

> people would tell me from the get-go what was wrong with it, why it was broken, why it was misoperative, why it was screwed up. I sat and I used to listen to that, and I thought, "What is this person learning from this dissing?" . . .
>
> When I was teaching at Bennington College there was a brilliant musician there who taught cello, George Finkel. . . . I went to a student concert—his first-year students. . . . It was the worst, most horrifying—I didn't know anything about cello, but I knew people were killing themselves. . . . People in the audience were staring at the ground and grimacing. . . .
>
> Finkel had his eyes closed and his head tilted back, and he was humming to himself—a big smile on his face. We walked out of there, and I said, "Wait a minute. . . . Not once did you flinch or grimace or groan. You taught these people, and they sounded like crap." He looked at me and he said, "Ah. After years of working with beginning students, you learn to listen for the good notes."
>
> Isn't that brilliant? . . . I got it then. If you look for what works, then your criticism has value. . . . If you can get people to see what works and why, and get them to expand that, then you've got a basis for criticism and improvement.

Cultivating the Attitude for Criticism

Chris Doerflinger of Elder Dance Express in Louisville, Kentucky, said,

> It's important to say what you have to say from the point of view of a friend. When you're criticizing, you only speak about *your* feelings, from your own experience, without passing judgment. "This is what I'm feeling."

No Personal Attacks

Some criticism comes from insecurity. If your criticism takes the form of a personal attack ("You never do this right!" "You are such a klutz!") rather than a response to the work, you are talking about your own insecurity, not the work.

Changing Negatives to Positives

When you perceive a problem, think through to a solution before you open your mouth. Give the performers directions without negatives. If it's too long, suggest a solution. ("Pick up the pace and energy level, and cut this section—you will intensify the build.") Change negative language to task language. ("Enter at this cue. Do your activity while you converse.")

Asking Questions

Instead of "You were late for your cue," ask, "What was going on at this point? What is your cue?" Instead of "You weren't paying attention to Sarah," try, "What were you paying attention to here?"

Receiving Criticism

Every artist needs to hear and absorb critical responses to his work, but it's hard to do.

When you receive criticism remind yourself that the subject is your performance, not you. Distance your ego from the discussion. Place your performance beside you and look at it as separate from yourself. Critical response is not about you; it is about your work.

No Argument

Listen quietly. Or use Active Listening. Instead of thinking up arguments: listen openly, reflect content, summarize, paraphrase, and ask clarifying questions. Let the ideas, positive and negative, get past your ego's defenses.

Formal Critical Processes That Work

A trick to giving constructive criticism is to decide what you want to achieve and frame your critique to attain your goal. Many people omit that first step, then express dismay when they set off booby traps. The people who have developed the following critical response processes have considered their goals in giving criticism.

Seeing, Feeling, Thinking Response

C. W. Metcalf developed a process to keep students from ripping into their peers during critiques. He asks them three questions: What did you see? What did you feel? What did you think?

Young performers don't know what they are getting across. They need to hear what they communicate. So the answer to the first question, "What did you see?" is a retelling of the action.

Student performers want to correct the audience narrative: "No, that's not what we did." Metcalf insists that they listen silently. If the audience's narrative doesn't jibe with the performer's concept, the performer concludes he needs to clarify part, or all, of his piece.

Next he asks, "What did you feel?" Viewers describe emotional and kinesthetic reactions and when they felt them. "I felt sad when you hung up the phone." "I was holding my breath the whole time you were tangled up."

The final question, "What did you think?" does not invite value judgments; it asks for ideas the respondents got from watching the piece. Some ideas may indicate how to improve it, where it could go, what it recalled; some might take it to the next step.

The seeing, feeling, thinking response teaches performers to take in audience response without defensive replies. It teaches respondents to speak of their experience of a piece without passing judgment down from on high. Once students acquire some performance skills, one-element criticism provides another useful response process.

One-Element Criticism

C. W. Metcalf introduced TOUCH to one-element criticism. The rule is, if we are working on one element, we critique only that element. If I ask a dancer to vary her dynamics, I critique only dynamics; I don't mention that she muffed the timing. When we work on timing I can critique timing.

One-element criticism allows performers to concentrate on one thing, which frees their creativity and makes it safe to experiment. It reins in the respondent's tendency to give too much feedback. It reduces the focus to a manageable chunk and allows for specificity in the work.

A pitfall of peer critiques is fear of the unfamiliar. If I see a performance that strikes me as strange, I may respond from fear, assume an attitude of superiority, and put it down. Neither fear nor superiority generate constructive criticism. When I find myself sitting in fear or feeling superior, I don't belong in the circle of respondents, because the goal of criticism is to improve the work.

The flip side of fear of the unknown is love of self—another pitfall. When I see someone else's work, I seek my own reflection there.

I like best that which reminds me of what I do, but my critique needs to help the artist do *her* best work, not *my* best work. My criticism is useless if I tell the artist how I would change her work so it would look more like what I like to do.

Liz Lerman's Critical Response Process

Liz Lerman struggled with these tendencies in herself. She realized that her most helpful critics understand the intention and form of her work; they see the work through the same frame Lerman looks through. Lerman has developed a critical response process that gives respondents the opportunity to learn about the work before they spout opinions. It gives control of the discussion to the artist. It requires the artist to think critically about what she wants to achieve in her work, and to frame questions which will give her the information she needs to achieve her ends.[19]

A facilitator can help people follow the steps in this process, clarify their responses, reframe questions, and stay on task.

Step One: Respondents Give Affirmations

In the first step, respondents give the performer affirmations. They state the significance of the work for them: what was meaningful or stimulating. They speak of specific positive elements—nothing generic, like "I loved it! It was great!" The more specific, the better: "I liked the way the repeated motif of the spirals built up the emotional intensity until the last one, which really moved me."

This step tells the artist what works, what is being communicated to the audience, and how. It melts her defensiveness and garners trust between her and the respondents.

Step Two: Performer Asks Questions

In the second step, the performer questions the respondents. This step encourages her to think critically about her work, and helps her get what she needs from the respondents. The questions can cover any topic: Do you understand the action? How do you interpret the symbology? How did you feel in this section? What do the costumes say to you? She can ask specific individuals to answer specific questions. She may want a dancer's response to the movement, and a writer's response to the text, for example.

Step Three: Respondents Ask Neutral Questions

In the third step, respondents ask the performer neutral questions. Lerman says, " . . . the actual process of trying to form opinions into neutral questions is precisely the process necessary to get to the questions that matter for the artist."[20] The search for neutrality helps the respondents deepen their thinking about the work, and helps the artist stay open to their feedback.

Respondents do not couch opinions in their questions. If a respondent feels a piece has no point, he cannot ask, "Why is there no point?" He could ask, "What do you want the audience to understand from your piece?" Here the performer receives information in a nonthreatening package. She could deduce that her meaning is unclear.

Step Four: Respondents Ask Permission to Give Opinions

In the fourth step, respondents ask the performer for permission to express their opinions on specific elements. "I have an opinion on the composition. Would you like to hear it?" The performer accepts or declines.

Ideally, by this time, the respondents have gained insight into her aesthetics and intentions. They fashion their opinions to help her achieve her goals, and do her best work, rather than to transform her piece into something they would create.

Asking the performer's permission before giving an opinion makes her the gatekeeper of the conversation. She can refuse opinions about aspects of the piece that aren't at issue for her, decline input about parts she knows how to improve, and end the giving of opinions on a specific element whenever she has heard enough.

Optional Step Five: Discussion of Content

If the respondents and the artist want to discuss the content or subject matter of a work, they do so here. If, during the previous steps, people get bogged down into content discussion, the facilitator can reassure them that they will discuss content issues after they get through the first four steps, and ask them to wait until then. If the content provokes intense controversy, and the respondents are hot to talk about it, the facilitator can ask the artist if she'd be willing to change the order of steps. If the artist agrees, they can skip from the first step to the fifth.

Optional Step Six: Discussion of Artist's Response

In this step, the artist can describe the path she plans to take to change her work in light of the responses she has heard. This step can give a sense of closing the circle of dialogue between artist and respondents.

Optional Step Seven: Work the Work

In the optional seventh step the artist and respondents get up and try their ideas in the studio.

Save It for the End of Rehearsal

Gerard Stropnicky of the Bloomsburg Theatre Ensemble said about Lerman's process that giving the performer control over the critiques she hears can backfire in an ongoing ensemble. If someone's opinion consistently gets turned down, or if someone has strong feelings about the work and cannot express them, the group will suffer.

> We know that two weeks after the show closes, you're going to have an opportunity to spout out anything you want. . . . If it's something like, "I hate what we're having to do in this scene; what does he think . . . ?" What we tell each other is, "Write it down. Save it for critique. Let it go." . . . And people do. . . . You know that there is a place . . . for those little or medium-sized artistic differences, you know there's a time to deal with it.

Formal Circle

Stropnicky described their critique process as a formal circle.

> This is what we would call a formal circle: Each person in the circle is invited to speak. They don't have to, but they're given permission to, and they must be heard, and they can talk uninterrupted for as long as they like. And then it moves on to the next person.
>
> After which it's a moderated discussion, where an outside eye or someone less involved in the whole project will run it and make sure everybody is heard until it's done. . . .
>
> The critique process is part of what keeps us sane. . . . Knowing that down the line there is a place where you can say this stuff. And for all of us, who are both directors and actors, it's very important to have that outlet.

Conflict Resolution

Attention to peaceful communication skills and adherence to constructive critical response processes will reduce the amount of conflict in any group. Nonetheless, conflict will happen. This section is about procedures for going through conflict in a healthy way.

What Causes Conflict?

Groups experience conflict for many reasons: when changes happen, when members have fundamentally different values, when the group doesn't meet the needs of its members, when status and power-sharing structures get fuzzy, when the group doesn't agree on normative behavior, when hidden agendas lurk, when cross-cultural communication breaks down, when prejudice and oppression infect a group.

Djola Branner, who, with Brian Freeman and Eric Gupton, founded Pomo Afro Homos (Postmodern African American Homosexuals), recalled experiencing conflict while the group worked out its power-sharing and decision-making norms:

> During our first show there were some problems that arose. We'd get to stalemates, and we'd have to decide who was going to get the final say-so, the director or the writer. And that was difficult and required a great deal of compromise. Sometimes I was happy; sometimes I wasn't. But it always became about surrendering control for the sake of the work.

Eight Successful Strategies for Resolving Conflict

A study of British string quartets found that successful groups use eight strategies to handle conflict about how to play a piece. All these strategies can help any collaborative group resolve conflict. If the conflict arises from general grumpiness, they table discussion until another day. In a second strategy they play one way for one concert and another way for another. A third approach gives the person playing the melody the choice about how to play. A fourth way makes it acceptable for a member not to concede if he feels strongly about an issue. A fifth strategy is to play much more than they talk; by playing they discover which way works best. In a sixth way quartet members implicitly agree to avoid areas of discussion that they know bear no fruit other than rancor. In a seventh, everyone recognizes that they share the same superordinate goal: to play the music as well as possible. Finally, they acknowledge that tension and conflict help the group explore music more deeply than if all agreed all the time. They value the creative potential of conflict.[21]

Conflict Is an Opportunity for Creativity and Growth

These successful string quartets know that conflict offers an opportunity for creativity and growth. If you can adjust your attitude about conflict to include interest in the process and hopefulness about its outcome, you have won half the battle.

Don't Bank Your Anger

Don't store up problems until you blow your stack. If you deal with issues as they arise, you have a better chance of creating peaceful solutions. It is easier to calmly express your annoyance over a small issue than to peacefully discuss something that has driven you crazy for months.

Letting your resentment pile up fills the atmosphere with tension. Your anger resonates and affects everyone around you, inhibiting creativity and disturbing community.

How Not to Set Up a Conflict

Marlene Johnson, a family and group therapist practicing in Atlanta, cautions:[22]

> Don't set up the conflict so that there has to be a winner and a loser; you are right and he is wrong; "It's mine and I want it"; you blame, shame or threaten; you must get an apology; you must be told you are good and have a right to walk the planet.

How to Set Up a Conflict

> Set it up so that you both can work on a problem together; you ask for his help on the problem; you gain understanding of his point of view; you combine your creativity to work it out; you both have a right to walk on the planet.

Get clear first about: How you feel. What you want. How you want it. When you want it.

Make an Appointment to Talk About It

Ask the other person when he can talk to you about the issue. "I'd like some time to talk about scheduling with you. When can we talk?"

Spend a few minutes centering yourself before the appointed time. Take deep breaths, release any tension you don't need, calm your mind. Give yourself an affirmation that will help you stay centered while you confront. Repeat the affirmation silently whenever you need to during the conversation.

Use I-Feel Statements

I-feel statements are a keystone of peaceful communication. People generally respond better to I-statements than to you-statements. They will react less defensively and more cooperatively. An I-feel statement has four parts:

1. I feel _____
2. When you _____
3. Because _____
4. And what I would like is _____.

I Feel . . . After "I feel," use one of five feeling words: *sad, mad, scared, hurt, happy*. These are the basic feelings, like the primary colors, which mix to create other feelings. I-feel statements are cleanest when you use one of the basic five. They keep the message simple.

Don't use words that blame the other person for your feelings: "I feel manipulated," or, "I feel dumped on." Those are verbs: you-statements in disguise. You may as well say, "You are dumping on me," and prepare for backlash.

When You . . . After "When you," briefly describe the behavior that bothers you. "When you leave your dishes in the sink." Or, "When you arrive twenty minutes late." Use neutral language. Do not judge or qualify or ascribe meaning or attitude to the behavior. "When you leave your filthy dishes in the sink" qualifies the dishes negatively ("filthy"). "When you act like a slob," is not specific enough and passes a negative judgment ("slob"). "When you thoughtlessly don't clean up after yourself," ascribes meaning to the behavior ("thoughtlessly"), and doesn't describe specific, observable behavior.

Because . . . After "Because," briefly explain how the behavior affects you. Frame it in terms of yourself. "Because I need the sink to cook dinner, and I don't have time to clean up your dishes and then cook." Or, "Because I like a clean kitchen."

Don't drag in morals, religion or rights, shoulds or oughts, generalizations or judgments. Not, "Because you should clean up after yourself." Not, "Because it's unsanitary." Not, "Because everybody knows that adults clean up their messes."

And What I Would Like Is . . . Here you describe specific, observable behavior you want from the other person. "And what I would like is for you to wash your dishes as soon as you finish eating, after every meal." Or, "And I would like you to clean your dishes before I get home every day." Say 100 percent of what you want.

Expect a Defensive Response, and Listen!

An I-feel statement constitutes the first step in conflict resolution: the confrontation. Ideally, the other person responds with, "Oh. OK." However, most people will respond defensively. Expect defensiveness. Get ready to shift into Active Listening. Listen fully to what the other person says: reflect, summarize, paraphrase. And then repeat your I-feel statement, word for word, if you like. You may cycle through this routine—I-feel statement, defensive response, and Active Listening—several times before you get to problem solving, which is the goal of confronting.

Define the Problem; Solve It Together

When the defensive response runs out of steam, agree on a definition of the problem. "The problem is that you don't have time to clean up after you eat, but I need a clean sink to cook, and I don't like washing your dishes." Figuratively move the problem out from between you and place it in front of both of you, or literally write it down and face it together. Then, brainstorm solutions.

When you finish brainstorming, list which ideas might work. Modify the most workable ideas until you can agree on one that seems good for both of you, one you both can try.

If it is important, you can write down the agreement, including who will do what, where, by when, and with what resources, and sign it. Make a date to evaluate and modify the solution. When you finish, give each other affirmations and evaluate the conflict resolution process.

How do you handle someone when he confronts by yelling, insulting, blaming, threatening—all those no-nos? First, don't actively listen to abuse. Acknowledge that he is upset. "You're really upset about this!" That acknowledgment may do the trick. His response may be, "You're #!*@#! right, I'm mad!" and then he might heave a sigh and start a calmer discussion. If he doesn't calm down enough for your comfort, assert that you won't listen to verbal abuse, but this is important and you want to talk later. Set a date, and leave.

If he is not too upset for you to handle, match him. Stand up, look him in the eye, and match his intensity by raising your voice somewhat, picking up your rhythm, and expanding your gestures. Then try to pace him back down to a comfortable energy level by gradually decreasing your intensity—sit down, lean back, take a deep breath, and lead him through a problem-solving process, as above.

Formal Conflict Resolution Processes

You can't always resolve a conflict, even when you are highly skilled in peaceful communication. If you try and fail, don't despair. You can use outside resources: mediation, facilitation, group therapy, formal negotiation, and individual therapy.

If you trust each other, have equal power in your relationship, and want to continue your relationship, mediation may help. A mediator is a trained, neutral third party who guides you through a conflict resolution process. The mediator does not solve your dispute, you do.

Several performing groups I interviewed have hired outside facilitators—group therapists, family therapists, or management experts—to help them resolve conflict. A facilitator enables a group to tackle tough issues by setting up a safe environment and leading people through a visioning or problem-solving process.

If your relationship has broken down and you no longer trust each other, you can hire a lawyer to negotiate for you. Formal negotiation presumes an adversarial relationship involving proposals and counterproposals. You ask for more than you want; she asks for more than she wants, and you chip away at each other's proposals until you reach an agreement. The process is slow, awkward, and expensive, but it can work as a last resort. It tends to destroy relationships, because it pits the two sides as opponents.

Finally, if you get into a conflict and try several different ways to resolve it without success, individual therapy may help you learn to live with the conflict. It could also lead you to discover that the conflict hurts too much and it has irreparably shattered your relationship. Therapy can help you through the difficulties of ending the relationship and moving on.

If you make a habit of choosing one skill to practice each time you find yourself in conflict, (to keep breathing throughout, or to summarize what you hear, for example) you can come out of every conflict with a sense of accomplishment, whether you get everything you want or not. If you approach every conflict as an opportunity for creativity and growth, you will create constructive solutions to disputes and grow in your ability to handle conflict.

Much conflict arises from poor communication. That is why peaceful communication practices will reduce the amount of conflict you encounter and will help you during conflict, so that your group's creativity can flourish.

In this book I have combined information from two separate processes—creative and collaborative. When I studied performing arts, I learned a great deal about creative process and nothing about group dynamics, yet I was expected to work in groups daily. Often I was surprised and dismayed when my work got bogged down in a dysfunctional group. Now I know that the more I use strategies like agreeing on guidelines and being open about power structures, the better my collaborations go, and the happier my collaborators are.

The information here about peaceful communication, constructive critiques, creating safety, power sharing, decision making, and group dynamics will make your studio a powerful and safe place, where you can make risky creative choices supported by the trust, respect, and love of your colleagues. The information about creative processes will open up new ways of following your creative impulses wherever they lead. I hope this book gives you the tools you need, and I wish for you the wildest, most wonderful, and most successful creative collaborations.

Notes

1. For this discussion of peaceful communication, I am indebted to Michel Avery, Brian Auvine, Barbara Streibel, Lonnie Weiss, *Building United Judgment: A Handbook for Consensus Decision Making*, (Madison, WI: The Center for Conflict Resolution, 1981), p. 14.

2. Ibid., p. 44.

3. Ibid., p. 21.

4. Hogie Wyckoff, *Solving Women's Problems Through Awareness, Action and Contact* (New York: Grove Press, 1977), p. 99.

5. For the following discussion of Active Listening, I am indebted to Dr. Thomas Gordon, *Leader Effectiveness Training: L.E.T., The No-Lose Way to Release the Productive Potential of People* (New York: P. H. Wyden Books, 1977).

6. Ibid., p. 66.

7. Ibid., p. 52.

8. Ibid., p. 60.

9. I am indebted to actor/teacher/playwright Sarah Froeber for my understanding of repetition. For a fuller description, see Sanford Meisner and Dennis Longwell, *Sanford Meisner on Acting,* with an introduction by Sydney Pollack (New York: Vintage Books, Random House, 1987).

10. Pierre Biner, *The Living Theatre* (New York: Horizon Press, 1972), pp. 81–88.

11. Virginia Satir, *Peoplemaking* (Palo Alto, CA: Science and Behavior Books, 1972), pp. 34–35.

12. Daniel Nagrin, *Dance and the Specific Image: Improvisation* (Pittsburgh, PA: University of Pittsburgh Press, 1994), pp. 13–14.

13. Kenneth D. Benne and Paul Sheats, "Functional Roles of Group Members," *Journal of Social Issues* 4 (spring 1948), 41–49, cited in Steven A. Beebe and John T. Masterson, *Communicating in Small Groups: Principles and Practices* (Glenview, IL: HarperCollins, 1989), pp. 64–65.

14. Ibid., pp. 93–99.

15. William J. J. Gordon, *Synectics: The Development of Creative Capacity* (New York: Collier Books, 1961), p. 68.

16. Keith Johnstone, *Impro! Improvisation and the Theatre,* with an introduction by Irving Wardle (London and Boston: Faber and Faber, 1979), pp. 101–102.

17. Marion O'Malley, *Advanced Conflict Resolution: Skill Building Workshop Manual* (Carrboro, NC: Center for Peace Education, 1994), p. 41.

18. Stephanie Judson, ed., Committee on Nonviolence and Children, Philadelphia Yearly Meeting of the Religious Society of Friends, *A Manual on Nonviolence and Children* (Philadelphia, PA: New Society, 1977), p. 13.

19. I am indebted to workshops with Liz Lerman as well as: Liz Lerman, "Toward a Process for Critical Response," *Alternate ROOTS* (spring 1993).

20. Ibid., p. 5.

21. J. Keith Murnighan and Donald E. Conlon, "The Dynamics of Intense Work Groups: A Study of British String Quartets," *Administrative Science Quarterly* 36 (1991), 177–8.

22. I am indebted to Marlene Johnson for much of the discussion of how to resolve a conflict.

Appendix A

Games and Exercises

affirmation circle, 93–94

aural image, 59

banging off the walls, 37–38

being together, 116

blind offers, 136

brainstorming, 10–11
  nominal group technique, 11
  rounds, 9–10

character motivation (I want, I need, I must), 58

character sketches, 34

character songs, 38

circles exercise, 37

complementary shapes, 53

concept statement, 47–48

contact improvisation, 119

creative choice games
  blind offers, 136
  energy catch, 118–19
  energy games, 15–16, 118
  I am a refrigerator, 136
  I've fallen, and I can't get up, 136–37
  protean catch, 6–7
  rounds, 9–10

dead-on-a-mat, 120

embodiment of atmosphere, 51

emotional subtext, 60

energy games, 15–16
  energy basics, 15
  energy bubble, 15
  energy catch, 118–19
  energy envelope, 15
  energy mirror, 16
  energy qualities, 16

essential sketches, 33–34

focus games
  focus ball toss, 66
  hocus-pocus, who's got the focus?, 66

free-writing, 22, 25

go somewhere, 20

harangues, 12–13

hocus-pocus, who's got the focus?, 66

hub meditation, 24–25

I am a refrigerator, 136

image exercise, 36–37

improvisation
  with object, 19
  one-word, 14
  silent, 14
  who, what, where, 14

impulse exercise, 11

incorporation of atmosphere, 51

I've fallen, and I can't get up, 136–37

killer monarch, 109

let me in! let me out!, 107

listen and respond around, 132

listening games
    listen for body language, 132
    listen for content, 132
    listen and respond around, 132
    repetition, 132
    seeing duet, 133
    toning the chord, 132
    total listening, 131
    true mirror, 133

make something
    make a mask, 19–20
    paint a painting, 19

meditation, 24
    hub meditation, 24–25

mindful chaos, 39

mirror games
    energy mirror, 16
    instant mirrors, 118
    leaderless mirror, 117
    oral mirror, 118
    true mirror, 133

mouse-in-the-house, 115

move, 18
    breathe and move to music, 18
    movement metaphors, 63
    movement phrase, 63–64
    moving together, 116

nominal group technique, 11

physicalization of psychological states, 63

play with objects, 18

protagonist and chorus, 61–62

protean catch, 6
    pass and change, 6
    pass and join in, 7

read someone else's writing, 22–23

repetition games, 132

rhythm and timing
    rhythm score, 64
    vocalize the rhythm of a sequence, 64

rhythmic excercise, 16–17

rounds, 9–10, 25

round-table discussion, 21–25

seeing duet, 133

sketches
    character sketches, 34
    essential sketches, 33–34
    sketching site-sculpture designs, 34–35

skill practice, 20

sound and movement, 119, 132

statues
    evolving, 13
    random, 13–14

storyboarding, 73

story pulling, 35–36

storytelling, 21, 25, 35

Story Theater, 31

surge, 115

toning the chord, 132

total listening, 131

travel as a group, 116

triangles, 109

true mirror, 133

trust games
    contact improv, 119
    dead-on-a-mat, 120
    trust circle, 120

try anything, 38–39

Appendix B

People I Interviewed

Robert A. Alexander, founding artistic director, Living Stage
Theatre Company, Washington, D.C.

Bill Allard, cofounder, performer, writer, Duck's Breath Mystery
Theater, San Francisco, Calif.

Steve Bailey, executive director, Jump-Start Performance
Company, San Antonio, Tex.

Eric Beatty, adjunct instructor, Department of Theatre, Towson
University; solo performer, Towson, Md.; former performer,
writer, Touchstone Theatre, Bethlehem, Pa.

Barbra Berlovitz Desbois, cofounder, coartistic director, Theatre
de la Jeune Lune, Minneapolis, Minn.

Laura Bertin, mime, Wayne, Pa.

Giles Blunden, architect; cofounder, Arcadia cohousing
community, Carrboro, N.C.

Martha Boesing, performer, Southern Theater, Minneapolis,
Minn.; dramaturg, director, A Traveling Jewish Theatre, San
Francisco, Calif.; founder, former artistic director, At the Foot
of the Mountain, Minneapolis, Minn.

Djola Branner, performer, writer, Minneapolis, Minn.; former
coartistic director, performer, writer, Pomo Afro Homos, San
Francisco, Calif.

Hilarie Burke-Porter, founding artistic director, writer, mime,
Silent Partners, Asheville, N.C.

Mark Butler, producer, videographer, Urban Media Group,
Swanton, Ohio.

Dan Chumley, codirector, writer, performer, San Francisco Mime Troupe, San Francisco, Calif.

Chip Dallery, M.S.W., family and emergency counselor, Philadelphia, Pa.

Dana Davis, dancer, mime, formerly with Silent Partners, Asheville, N.C.

Babs Davy, codirector, performer, writer, Five Lesbian Brothers, Brooklyn, N.Y.

Judith DeWitt, dancer, choreographer, Chattanooga, Tenn.; former assistant director, choreographer, company member, The Dance Unit, Atlanta, Ga.

Dominique Dibbell, codirector, performer, writer, Five Lesbian Brothers, New York, N.Y.

Mary Dino, performer, creator, Bond Street Theatre Coalition, New York, N.Y.

Chris Doerflinger, choreographer, director, Elder Dance Express; physical education teacher, Jefferson County Youth Detention Center, Louisville, Ky.

Gail Dottin, performer, writer, AwarenessAct, Brooklyn, N.Y.

Ariel Dubiner, freelance actor.

Robert Francesconi, assistant dean, School of Drama, North Carolina School of the Arts, Winston-Salem, N.C.

Gwylène Gallimard, site installation artist, Charleston, S.C.

Richard Geer, president, Community Performance; artistic director: Swamp Gravy, Colquitt, Ga.; City Bridges, Newport News, Va.; Scrap Mettle SOUL, Chicago, Ill.; Grit and Grace, Walton County, Fla.

Adam Gertsacov, clown, director, writer, Acme Clown Company, Providence, R.I.

Jenny Gilrain, ensemble member, Touchstone Theatre, Bethlehem, Pa.

D. Scott Glasser, director, Madison Repertory Theatre, Madison, Wis.; former actor, writer, Dakota Theatre Caravan

Diana Gore, educator/performer, AwarenessAct, Brooklyn, N.Y.

Darby Hayes, mime, corporate trainer, Coconut Grove, Fla.

Keith Hennessy, performer, creator, Contraband, San Francisco, Calif.

Jyl Hewston, lecturer, Department of Theatre, Film and Dance, Humboldt State University, Arcata, Calif.; former mime, writer, codirector, Theatre Plexus, Takoma Park, Md.; writer, actor, director, Howling Woolf Theatre, Arcata, Calif.

Lin Hixson, director, Goat Island performance group, Chicago, Ill.

Sterling Houston, artistic director, Jump-Start Performance Company, San Antonio, Tex.

Sharon Jane, member, WOW Café, New York, N.Y.

Jef, cofounder, producing director, Jelly Educational Theater, Carrboro, N.C.; cofounder, former codirector, mime, creator, TOUCH Mime Theater, Carrboro, N.C.

Marlene Johnson, group and individual radical therapist, Atlanta, Ga.

Tom Keegan, cofounder, codirector, performer, writer, Keegan and Lloyd, Santa Monica, Calif.

Steven Kent, freelance director, Los Angeles, Calif.; director, The Institute for Conscious Acting, University of La Verne, La Verne, Calif.; former member, Company Theatre; former director, Provisional Theatre, Los Angeles, Calif.

Karen Kimbrel, executive director, Colquitt Miller County Arts Council, Swamp Gravy, Colquitt, Ga.

Christine Lassiter, poet, playwright, Asheville, N.C.

Robert Leonard, associate professor, Department of Theatre Arts, Virginia Tech, Blacksburg, Va.; founder, former co-artistic director, the Road Company, Johnson City, Tenn.

Liz Lerman, founder, artistic director, choreographer, Liz Lerman Dance Exchange, Takoma Park, Md.

Francisco Letelier, community muralist, Los Angeles, Calif.

William Liles, Senior Scientist, Central Intelligence Agency, Washington, D.C.

Davidson Lloyd, cofounder, codirector, performer, writer, Keegan and Lloyd, Santa Monica, Calif.

Andrew Long, cofounder, choreographer, Johnson/Long Dance Company, Austin, Tex.

Ruth Maleczech, founding coartistic director, Mabou Mines, New York, N.Y.

Jeff Mather, community site sculptor, Atlanta, Ga.

Michael McGuigan, performer, writer, musician, Bond Street Theatre Coalition, New York, N.Y.

Mark McKenna, artistic director, ensemble member, Touchstone Theatre, Bethlehem, Pa.

C. W. Metcalf, corporate trainer, Liten Up, Idyllwild, Calif.; former mime, creator, director, Mad Mountain Mime; director, Magic Mountain Mime School, Tallahassee, Fla.

Barry Mines, former director, Lime Kiln Arts, Lexington, Va.

Hardin Minor, coartistic director, OMIMEO Mime Theatre; president, Mime in Motion, Charlotte, N.C.

Tony Montanaro, mime, director, teacher, Portland, Me.; former artistic director, Celebration Mime Theatre; Celebration Mime School, South Paris, Me.

Christine Murdock, former senior ensemble member, co−artistic director, the Road Company, Johnson City, Tenn.

Leslie Neal, choreographer, artistic director, Art Spring, associate professor of dance, Florida International University, former artistic director, Leslie Neal Dance, Miami, Fla.

Naomi Newman, cofounder, codirector, actor, A Traveling Jewish Theatre, San Francisco, Calif.

John O'Neal, founding director, actor, Junebug Productions, New Orleans, La.; former member, Free Southern Theatre, Jackson, Miss. and New Orleans, La.

Judy Panetta, former director, Stageworks Touring Company, Glassboro, N.J.

Bob Paton, founder, director, Theatre of Dreams; former member, Living Theatre; Playback Theatre, New York, N.Y.

Linda Probus, M.A., A.T.R. individual, group, and emergency therapist, Louisville, Ky.

David Reiffel, composer, People's Opera Company, Boston, Mass.; former composer, musician, Cornerstone Theater Company, Santa Monica, Calif.

Joan Schirle, coartistic director, performer, The Dell'Arte Company, director of training, The Dell'Arte International School of Physical Theatre, Blue Lake, Calif.

Sue Schroeder, choreographer, artistic director, CORE Performance Company, Decatur, Ga.

Joanna Sherman, cofounder, artistic director, Bond Street Theatre Coalition, New York, N.Y.

Deborah Slater, choreographer, artistic director, Art of the Matter, Sausalito, Calif.

Gerard Stropnicky, actor, codirector, Bloomsburg Theatre Ensemble, Bloomsburg, Pa.

Ruth Tamir, freelance performer.

Carlos Uriona, actor/managing director, Double Edge Theatre, Ashfield, Mass.; founding codirector, Diablomundo, Buenos Aires, Argentina.

Barbara Vann, coartistic director, Medicine Show Theatre Ensemble; former company member, The Open Theatre, New York, N.Y.

Shelley Wallace, mime, creator, Jest in Time Theatre, Halifax, Nova Scotia, Canada; former mime, Celebration Mime Theatre, South Paris, Me.

Ann Weisman, performance poet, Lawton, Okla.

Allen Welty-Green, composer, musician, Gnosis, Axis, Atlanta, Ga.

Jerita Wright, cofounder, director, Carolina Artists and Thespians, Asheville, N.C.

⬛ibliography

ADLER, STELLA. 1988. *The Technique of Acting*. Toronto and New York: Bantam Books.

ALEXANDER, ROBERT. 1983. *Improvisational Theatre for the Classroom: A Curriculum Guide for Training Regular and Special Education Teachers in the Art of Improvisational Theatre*. Edited by Wendy Haynes. Washington, DC: Living Stage/Arena Stage.

AVERY, MICHEL, BARBARA STREIBEL, BRIAN AUVINE, AND LONNIE WEISS. 1981. *Building United Judgment: A Handbook for Consensus Decision Making*. Madison, WI: The Center for Conflict Resolution.

BARKER, CLIVE. 1977. *Theatre Games: A New Approach to Drama Training*. London: Eyre Methuen.

BEEBE, STEVEN A., AND JOHN T. MASTERSON. 1989. *Communicating in Small Groups: Principles and Practices*. Glenview, IL: HarperCollins.

BELT, LYNDA, AND REBECCA STOCKLEY. 1991. *Improvisation Through TheatreSports*. Seattle, WA: Thespis Productions.

BINER, PIERRE. 1972. *The Living Theatre*. New York: Horizon Press.

BLOM, LYNNE ANNE, AND L. TARIN CHAPLIN. 1982. *The Intimate Act of Choreography*. Pittsburgh, PA: University of Pittsburgh Press.

BOAL, AUGUSTO. 1992. *Games for Actors and Non-Actors*. Translated by Adrian Jackson. New York: Routledge.

———. 1979. *Theater of the Oppressed*. Translated by Charles A. and Maria-Odilia Leal McBride. New York: Urizen Books.

BROWN, RICHARD P., ed. 1972. *Actor Training 1*. New York: Institute for Research in Acting with Drama Book Specialists.

BROWN, RITA MAE. 1976. *A Plain Brown Rapper*. Illus. Sue Sellars. Oakland, CA: Diana Press.

BROYLES-GONZÁLEZ, YOLANDA. 1994. *El Teatro Campesino: Theater in the Chicano Movement*. Austin, TX: University of Texas Press.

BUTLER, C. T. LAWRENCE, AND AMY ROTHSTEIN. 1991. *On Conflict and Consensus: A Handbook on Formal Consensus Decisionmaking.* Portland, ME: Food Not Bombs.

CAMERON, JULIA. 1992. *The Artist's Way: A Spiritual Path to Higher Creativity.* New York: G. P. Putnam's Sons.

CARNEGIE, DALE. 1940. *How to Win Friends and Influence People.* New York: Pocket Books.

CHAIKIN, JOSEPH. 1972. *The Presence of the Actor.* New York: Theatre Communications Group.

CLARK, BRIAN. 1971. *Group Theatre.* London: Pitman.

COLLISON, WILLIAM. 1988. *Conflict Reduction: Turning Conflict to Cooperation.* Dubuque, IA: Kendall/Hunt.

DAVIS, R. G. 1975. *The San Francisco Mime Troupe: The First Ten Years.* Palo Alto, CA: Ramparts Press.

DE BONO, EDWARD. 1970. *Lateral Thinking: Creativity Step by Step.* New York: Harper and Row.

———. 1985. *Six Thinking Hats.* Boston: Little, Brown.

DELL, CECILY. 1977. *A Primer for Movement Description Using Effort-Shape and Supplementary Concepts.* New York: Dance Notation Bureau Press.

FELDENKRAIS, MOSHÉ. 1977. *Awareness Through Movement: Health Exercises for Personal Growth.* New York: Harper and Row.

FLUEGELMAN, ANDREW, ed., New Games Foundation. 1976. *The New Games Book.* Garden City, NY: Doubleday.

FROEBER, SARAH, 2000. *Melvin the Pelican.* Music by Mike Hamer, lyrics by Sarah Froeber and Mike Hamer. Woodstock, IL: Dramatic.

GERTSACOV, ADAM. 1990. "The One Sure Thing: A Cabaret on Death." Master's thesis, Rhode Island College.

GHISELIN, BREWSTER, ed. 1952. *The Creative Process.* New York and Toronto: New American Library (Mentor).

GOLDBERG, NATALIE. 1986. *Writing Down the Bones: Freeing the Writer Within.* Boston and London: Shambhala.

GOLEMAN, DANIEL. 1995. *Emotional Intelligence.* New York: Bantam Books.

GOLEMAN, DANIEL, PAUL KAUFMAN, AND MICHAEL RAY. 1992. *The Creative Spirit*. New York: Dutton.

GORDON, THOMAS. 1977. *Leader Effectiveness Training: L.E.T., The No-Lose Way to Release the Productive Potential of People*. New York: P. H. Wyden Books.

GORDON, WILLIAM J. J. 1968. *Synectics: The Development of Creative Capacity*. New York: Collier Books.

HAGEN, UTA. 1973. *Respect for Acting*. New York: Macmillan.

HALL, EDWARD T. 1973. *The Silent Language*. Garden City, NY: Anchor/Doubleday.

————. 1977. *Beyond Culture*. Garden City, NY: Anchor/Doubleday.

HALPRIN, LAWRENCE, AND JIM BURNS, WITH CONTRIBUTIONS BY ANNA HALPRIN AND PAUL BAUM. 1974. *Taking Part: A Workshop Approach to Collective Creativity*. Cambridge, MA: MIT Press.

HENLEY, NANCY M. 1977. *Body Politics: Power, Sex, and Nonverbal Communication*. Englewood Cliffs, NJ: Prentice-Hall.

HUANG, KERSON, AND ROSEMARY HUANG. 1987. *I Ching*. New York: Workman.

HUMPHREY, DORIS. 1959. *The Art of Making Dances*. ed. Barbara Pollack. New York: Rinehart.

JANIS, IRVING L. 1971. "Groupthink." *Psychology Today* 5 (November).

JOHNSON, DAVID W., AND FRANK P. JOHNSON. 1975. *Joining Together: Group Theory and Group Skills*. Englewood Cliffs, NJ: Prentice-Hall.

JOHNSTONE, KEITH. 1979. *Impro! Improvisation and the Theatre*. London and Boston: Faber and Faber.

JUDSON, STEPHANIE, comp. and ed., Committee on Nonviolence and Children, Philadelphia Yearly Meeting of the Religious Society of Friends. 1977. *A Manual on Nonviolence and Children*. Philadelphia, PA: New Society.

KOESTLER, ARTHUR. 1964. *The Act of Creation*. New York: MacMillan.

LABAN, RUDOLF, AND F. C. LAWRENCE. 1974. *Effort*. Plymouth, England: MacDonald and Evans.

LERMAN, LIZ. 1993. "Toward a Process for Critical Response." *Alternate ROOTS* (spring).

LESSAC, ARTHUR. 1981. *Body Wisdom: The Use and Training of the Human Body.* New York: Drama Book Specialists.

LEWIS, HOWARD R., AND DR. HAROLD S. STREITFELD. 1972. *Growth Games: How to Tune in Yourself, Your Family, Your Friends.* New York: Bantam Books.

LIEBERMAN, MORTON A., IRVIN D. YALOM, AND MATTHEW B. MILES. 1973. *Encounter Groups: First Facts.* New York: Basic Books.

LONDON, TODD. 1991. "Gentle Revolutionaries." *American Theatre* (July/August).

MACBETH, JESSICA. 1990. *Moon over Water: The Path of Meditation.* Bath, England: Gateway Books.

MAURER, RICHARD E. 1991. *Managing Conflict; Tactics for School Administrators.* Boston: Allyn and Bacon.

MEISNER, SANFORD, AND DENNIS LONGWELL. 1987. *Sanford Meisner on Acting.* New York: Random House.

METCALF, C. W. 1976. *The BodySong.* Unpublished manuscript.

MONTANARO, TONY, WITH KAREN HURLL MONTANARO. 1995. *Mime Spoken Here: The Performer's Portable Workshop.* Gardiner, ME: Tilbury House.

MORENO, JACOB L. 1983. *The Theatre of Spontaneity.* Ambler, Pa.: Beacon House.

MORGENROTH, JOYCE. 1987. *Dance Improvisations.* Pittsburgh, PA: University of Pittsburgh Press.

MURNIGHAN, J. KEITH, AND DONALD E. CONLON. 1991. "The Dynamics of Intense Work Groups: A Study of British String Quartets." *Administrative Science Quarterly* 36.

Music Lovers' Encyclopedia. 1954. Edited by Deems Taylor and Russell Kerr from materials compiled by Rupert Hughes. Garden City, NY: Doubleday.

NAGRIN, DANIEL. 1994. *Dance and the Specific Image: Improvisation.* Pittsburgh, PA: University of Pittsburgh Press.

O'MALLEY, MARION. 1994. *Advanced Conflict Resolution: Skill Building Workshop Manual.* Carrboro, NC: Center for Peace Education.

ORLICK, TERRY. 1978. *Winning Through Cooperation.* Washington, DC: Acropolis Books.

PASOLLI, ROBERT. 1970. *A Book on the Open Theatre.* New York: Avon.

PAVITT, CHARLES. 1993. "What (Little) We Know About Formal Group Discussion Procedures." *Small Group Research* (London) 24 (2).

RIBNER, SUSAN, AND RICHARD CHIN. 1984. *The Martial Arts.* New York: Harper and Row.

ROTHENBERG, ALBERT. 1979. *The Emerging Goddess: The Creative Process in Art, Science, and Other Fields.* Chicago: University of Chicago Press.

SARTRE, JEAN-PAUL. 1957. *No Exit and Three Other Plays.* New York: Vintage Books.

SATIR, VIRGINIA. 1972. *Peoplemaking.* Palo Alto, CA: Science and Behavior Books.

SCHECHNER, RICHARD. 1973. *Environmental Theater.* New York: Hawthorn Books.

SCHUTZ, WILLIAM C. 1982. *Elements of Encounter.* New York: Irvington.

SPOLIN, VIOLA. 1985. *Improvisation for the Theater: A Handbook of Teaching and Directing Techniques.* Evanston, IL: Northwestern University Press.

STANISLAVSKI, CONSTANTIN. 1964. *An Actor Prepares.* Translated by Elizabeth Reynolds Hapgood. New York: Routledge.

————. 1977. *Building a Character.* Translated by Elizabeth Reynolds Hapgood. New York: Theatre Arts Books.

————. 1961. *Creating a Role.* Translated by Elizabeth Reynolds Hapgood. New York: Theatre Arts Books.

SWEET, JEFFREY. 1993. *The Dramatist's Toolkit: The Craft of the Working Playwright.* Portsmouth, NH: Heinemann.

TOLKIEN, J. R. R. 1991. Illustrated by Alan Lee. *The Lord of the Rings.* Boston: Houghton Mifflin.

WEINSTEIN, MATT, AND JOEL GOODMAN. 1980. *PlayFair: Everybody's Guide to Noncompetitive Play.* San Luis Obispo, CA: Impact.

WYCKOFF, HOGIE. 1976. *Love, Therapy and Politics: Issues in Radical Therapy—The First Year.* New York: Grove Press.

————. 1977. *Solving Women's Problems Through Awareness, Action and Contact.* New York: Grove Press.

WYNN, RICHARD, AND CHARLES W. GUDITUS. 1984. *Team Management: Leadership by Consensus.* Columbus, OH: Merrill.

Index

Active Listening, 124, 127–30
  in conflict, 148
  definition, 124
  during critique, 140
Actor Training 1, 115
Aesop, 51
affirmation
  circle, 93
  in conflict, 149
  in critique, 142
  to erase negative thoughts, 127
Ailey, Alvin, 65
Alexander, Robert, 20
Alexander technique, 79
Allard, Bill, 4, 7, 22, 39, 56
Allen, Steve, 22
American Beauty, 54
Archetypal states, 111–12
Aristotle, 42, 55
assumptions
  element of composition, 54
  questions about, 30
  underlying, 54
atmosphere
  as central element of composition,
    49–51
  embodiment of, 51
  incorporation of, 51
  resentment and, 85, 146
  unsafe, 114
At the Foot of the Mountain
    Theatre, 35, 87, 90, 101, 110
audience
  affecting, 52
  as central element of composition,
    52–53
  to complete a work, 81

genre and, 41–42
mission and, 52
questions about, 30
symbols and, 54–55
aural image exercise, 59
aural statement, 65
AwarenessAct, 8

banging off the walls, 37–38
beats, 66
Beatty, Eric, 19
Beckett, Samuel, 54
Beebe, Steven, 133, 135
beginning, middle, and end
  beats and, 43
  breaking material into, 42
  movement phrases and,
    63–64
being together game, 116
Belt, Lynda, 14
Berlovitz Desbois, Barbra, 103
Berne, Eric, 123
Bertin, Laura, 24
blackboard, 71
Blacklight Theatre of Prague, 54
blind offers game, 136
blocking
  character and, 61
  clarity and, 65
  diagram, 61
  focus and, 66
  relationship and, 61
  status and, 61
Bloomsburg Theatre Ensemble, 34,
    73, 79, 92, 103–04, 138, 144
Blue Man Group, 8, 54
body language, 58–59, 126

Boesing, Martha, 35, 87, 90, 110
Bond Street Theatre Coalition, 21, 41
boundary between art and therapy, 87–88
brainstorm
  in conflict, 148
  how to, 10–11
  nominal group technique, 11
  rounds, 9–10
  in script writing, 75
Branner, Djola, 74, 93, 145
Brown, Rita Mae, 114
build, 43, 67
Burke-Porter, Hilarie, 23

Cabaret on Death, A. See *One Sure Thing, The*
Campbell, Joseph, 23
cards on the floor, 73
Celebration Barn, 3
Center for Peace Education, 137
Chaikin, Joseph, 78–79, 132
character
  aural image of, 59
  body language, 58–59
  conflict and, 55
  development, 43–44, 57
  dressing as, 7
  element of composition, 57–58
  emotional subtext, 60
  epiphany and, 56
  genre and, 41
  in commedia dell'arte, 41
  internal world of, 59
logic and, 43
  motivation, 58
  negotiating over object, 60
  physicalization of, 58–59
  point of view and, 19, 57
  questions about, 30–31
  relationships, 61
character sketches, 34
character songs, 38
check-ins, 90–91
check-outs, 93
Children of a Lesser God, 57

choreographer
  Ailey, Alvin, 65
  DeWitt, Judith, 18
  Doerflinger, Chris, 139
  Humphrey, Doris, 53–61
  Jones, Bill T., 43
  Lerman, Liz, 29, 60, 63, 80, 102–03, 142–44
  Long, Andrew, 19, 77
  Morris, Leslie, 18
  Nagrin, Daniel, 14, 24, 37, 77, 133
  Paxton, Steve, 119
  Schroeder, Sue, 19, 92
choreography, 62–65
Chrietzberg, Susan, 53
Christopher, Karen, 20
Chumley, Dan, 31, 101
circles exercise, 37
clarity, 65–66
Clark, Brian, 38, 79
climax
  dynamic build to, 43
  epiphany at, 56
Coffey, Dan, 22
collaboration
  beauty of, 95
  conflict and, 145–46
  consensus and, 96–100
  directors and, 101, 102–04
  joy of, xi–xii, 10
  on mission statement, 51–52
  open mind and, 95
  power struggles and, 126
  with tech team, 67
collaborative writing techniques, 74–76
collective
  anarchist, 78, 92
  feminist, 114
collectives
  At the Foot of the Mountain, 35, 87, 90, 101
  Bloomsburg Theatre Ensemble, 34, 73, 79, 92
  Bond Street Theatre Coalition, 21, 41
  Company Theatre, 35, 101

Contraband, 78, 81, 92
Diablomundo, 81, 108
Furies, 114
Living Theatre, 101
San Francisco Mime Troupe, 101
comedy
Aristotelian, 42
blocking and, 61
climax and, 43
Cosby, Bill, 8
Duck's Breath Mystery Theater,
4–5, 7, 22, 39, 56
element of composition, 56–57
Five Lesbian Brothers, 5, 14, 21,
22, 71, 91
as genre, 41–42
juxtaposition and, 56–57
opposition and, 55–56
questions about, 30
situation, 42
stand up, 42
surprise and, 57
timing and, 64
commedia dell'arte, 41, 42
Communicating in Small Groups, 133
communication
Active Listening, 127–31
in conflict, 123, 127–31, 145–50
constructive critiques, 138–44
defensive, 135
evaluative, 137–38
group maintenance, 133–35
guidelines for peaceful, 124–26
listening games, 131–33
nonverbal, 58–59, 126, 128
peaceful, 123–33
with self, 126–27
supportive, 135
Company Theatre, 35, 101
complementary shapes game, 53
concept
atmosphere and, 49–50
central element, 47
statement, 47–48
super-ogre and, 95
conflict, dramatic
as element of composition, 55

opposition and, 55–56
questions about, 30
conflict, in a group
anger in, 146
check-ins and, 91
check-outs and, 93
consensus and, 97, 99
facilitation of, 149
group cycles and, 116–17
mediation of, 149
naming behavior in, 111, 113
negotiation of, 149–50
peaceful resolution of, 145–50
power struggles and, 124,
126
setting up, 146–48
strategies for, 145–46
consensus decision making
flow chart, 100
guidelines for, 124
how it works, 96–100
if agreement doesn't happen,
99
roles, 97–99
vocabulary, 99
contact improvisation, 119–20
Contraband, 78, 81, 92, 102
copyright, 86
CORE Performance Company, 19, 92
Cornerstone Theater Company, 22,
75, 96
Cosby, Bill, 8
costume
audience and, 52
file ideas for, 28
genre and, 41
as initial idea, 67
world and, 54
creative choice games
blind offers, 136
energy catch, 118–19
energy games, 15–16, 118–19
I am a refrigerator, 136
I've fallen and I can't get up,
136–37
protean catch, 6–7
rounds, 9–10

creative process
  chance and, 5–6
  failures and, 3–5
  getting stuck in, 76–79
  no order in, 26
  one-element-at-a-time, 28–29,
    45–67
  in one paragraph, 80
  questions for, 30–31, 67
  safety and, 86–87
  stories as source for, 21
  time and, 81
  TV and radio as source, 23
  web of composition, 47–49
  when it is over, 81
creativity
  collaboration and, xi–xii
  in conflict resolution, 146–48
  details and, 45–46
  fostering, 6–7, 86–87
  meditation and, 24
  one-element-criticism and, 141
  playing and, 6–7
  supportiveness and, 136
  in Synectics, 136
critical response processes, 138–44
criticism, negative, 140
critique, constructive
  definition, 138
  guidelines for, 138–40
  receiving, 140
  See also evaluation
cutting, 79–80

Dakota Theatre Caravan, 32, 76, 138
Dance and the Specific Image, 24
Dance Exchange, Liz Lerman, 29, 60,
    80, 102–03
Dance Unit, The, 18
Davis, R. G., 31, 101
Davy, Babs, 5, 14
dead-on-a-mat exercise, 120
dead horse, 76
decision making
  conflict over, 79–80, 96
  by consensus, 96–100
  about cutting, 79–80

  by director, 102–104
  by rotating ogreship, 94–96
  statement as guide for, 51–52
  by those who take action, 108
  and writing down decisions, 29
Dell'Arte International School, The,
    40, 115
Dell'Arte Company, The, 67, 74
"D-Man in the Water", 43
denouement, 43
design in space and time, 53
details
  in beat-to-beat, 67
  to free creativity, 45–46
  in image exercise, 36
DeWitt, Judith, 18
Diablomundo, 81, 108
Dibbell, Dominique, 14
Doerflinger, Chris, 139
Donlon, James, 114
Don't Drop Grandma, 19
Double Edge Theatre, 81
Dramatist's Toolkit, The, 60
dreams
  for getting unstuck, 76, 78
  as idea source, 23
  myth and, 23
dream world, 54
Duck's Breath Mystery Theater, 4–5,
    7, 22, 39, 56
dynamics
  of body language, 58–59
  definition of, 64
  as element of composition, 64–65
  of opposition, 55–56
  rhythmic exercise, 16–17
  of stage picture, 61
dynamics, group
  definition of, 106
  over time, 116
  of roles people play, 110–13
  of victim/persecutor/rescuer cycle,
    112

editing. *See* cutting
Elder Dance Express, 139
elements of composition

central, 47–53
  choosing one to work on, 45–46
  illustrations, 48, 49
  supporting, 54–67
  web of composition, 48, 49
elephant in the living room, 113
El Teatro Campesino, 53
emotion
  body language and, 58
  group atmosphere and, 85
  harangues and, 13
  timing, rhythm, and, 64
emotional experience
  as idea source, 25
  validating, 119
emotional subtext, 60
emotions in a group
  acknowledging, 87–119
  check-ins, 90–91
  check-outs, 93
  in conflict, 145–49
  empath and, 98
  fear, 3–5, 87, 141
  gaining power with, 107–108
  I-feel statement, 124
  reflecting, 132, 133
  safety and, 87
  strong feelings, 125
  trust games and, 119
end
  of creative process, 41
  -of-rehearsal critique, 144
energy
  basics, 15
  body language and, 58–59
  bubble or envelope, 15
  choreography and, 62
  dynamics and, 64
  ensemble building and, 16
  idea source, 15
  mirror, 16
  qualities, 16
  in triangles game, 109–10
  in warm-up, 92
energy catch game, 118–19
ensemble
  AwarenessAct, 8

Bloomsburg Theatre, 34, 73, 79,
  92, 103–04, 138, 144
  Medicine Show Theatre, 13, 38,
  63
ensemble building
  chatting and, 91
  energy and, 16
environment
  of safety in rehearsal, 85–90
  See also atmosphere
epiphany, 56
essential sketches, 33–34
evaluation
  after brainstorm 10–11
  after conflict resolution, 149
  group maintenance, 134, 137–38
  of peers, 137–38
  of rehearsal, 93
  versus critique, 138

facilitation, 97–99, 142, 149
failure
  accepting, 89
  in conflict resolution, 149–50
  fear of, 3–5
  to reach consensus, 99–100
fairy tales, 37–38
fear, 87
feelings. See emotions
file, for an idea, 28
Five Lesbian Brothers, 5, 14, 21, 22,
  71, 91
flag on the play, 89
focus
  aid to clarity, 66
  definition of, 66
  as element of composition, 66
  games
    ball toss, 66
    energy catch, 118
    hocus-pocus, 66
    mouse in the house, 115
Foreman, Ronlin, 115
form
  choosing, 41
  element of choreography, 62
  and structure, 40–44

formal circle critique, 144
format, working, 29
Francesconi, Bob, 16
Freeman, Brian, 145
Free Southern Theatre, 52
free-writing, 22, 25
Friends, Religious Society of,
        123–25, 138
Froeber, Sarah, 40
Furies Collective, 114

games and exercises. *See*
        Appendix A, 153
genre
    atmosphere and, 50
    audience and, 41–42
    choosing, 41
    definition, 41
    list of genres, 42
    spiritual beliefs and, 42
Gertsacov, Adam, 72, 85, 88
Ghandi, Mahatma, 123
Glasser, D. Scott, 32, 138
Goat Island performance group, 20,
        102
Gordon, Dr. Thomas, 127
Gore, Diana, 8
going somewhere, idea source,
        20
Goulish, Matthew, 20
Grand Union, 119
graphics, 65
Gray, Paul, 58
ground rules. *See* guidelines
group
    behaviors, 106–21
    cohesion-building games, 107,
        109, 115, 116, 117–19
    communication, 85–94, 133–35
    conflict in, 123–26, 145–50
    consensus, 96–100, 124–26
    creativity, 6, 9–11, 86–87
    cycles, 113, 116–17
    dynamics, 106–21
    evaluation, 137–38
    guidelines for a, 85–90, 124–26
    maintenance, 133–35

    power in a, 107–10
    roles people play in, 110–13
    therapy, 95–96, 149
    trust building games, 119–20
Group Theatre, 38, 79
groupthink, 113
guidelines
    for consensus groups, 124–26
    for safe groups, 85–90
Gupton, Eric, 145

Hakoshima, Yass, 15
harangue, 12–13
Hayes, Darby, 77, 131
Hennessy, Keith, 78, 81, 92, 102
Hewston, Jyl, 19, 21, 75
history lectures, 31
Hixson, Lin, 20
hocus-pocus, who's got the focus?, 66
Horsepower, 33
Howling Woolf Theatre, 19, 75–76
hub meditation, 24
Humphrey, Doris, 53, 61

I am a refrigerator game, 136
ideas
    "brilliant," 7–8, 26, 45–46
    central, 47
    choosing, 7–8
    generating material about, 28–39
    how to talk about, 25–26
    initial, 7–8
    lack of, 3–4
    trying everyone's, 90
    where to get them, 3–8, 9–26
image
    and audience, 52
    aural, 59
    central, 47–49
    design in space and time and, 53
    hub meditation and, 24–25
    impulse exercise and, 11–12
    as visual statement, 65
image exercise, 36–37, 59
imagination, 20–21
improvisation
    with breath, 18

contact improv, 119–20
  as idea source, 17, 18, 25
  as negotiation over object, 60
  nonverbal, 14
  one-word, 14
  to find design in time, 53
  who, what, where, 14
  with objects, 18–19
  See also Appendix A, 153
improvisational
  poetry and stories, 20
  structures, inventing, 29
Improvisation for the Theater, 14, 117
impulse exercise, 11–12
Inferno, 54
inspiration, 3–4, 8
Institute for Urban Arts, 33
interviews, 32–33
I-statements, 124, 147
I've fallen and I can't get up! game,
  136–37

Janis, Irving, 113
Jef, ix, 18, 23, 76, 77, 89, 136
Jest in Time Theatre, 21, 125
Johnson/Long Dance Company, 19,
  77
Johnson, Marlene, 93, 146–48
Johnstone, Keith, 14, 109, 136
Jones, Bill T., 43
Judson Dance Theater, 119
Junebug Productions, 52, 104
Just One of Those Days, 47, 50
juxtaposition, 25, 56–57

Keegan and Lloyd, 25, 37–38, 77, 80,
  89
Keegan, Tom, 25, 37–38, 77, 89
Kent, Steven, 35, 43, 70, 78, 87, 90,
  95, 107–08
Kessler, Merle, 7
killer monarch game, 109
kill the leader, 114–15
kinesthetic
  awareness, 115–16
  reactions, 141
King, Dr. Martin Luther, Jr., 123

Kupers, Terry, 95, 107
Lab time, 92
Leader Effectiveness Training, 127
Leading and following skills, 17,
  115–16, 117–18, 136
LeCoq, Jacques, 61
Lerman, Liz, 29, 60, 63, 80, 102–03,
  142–44
  critical response process, 142–44
let me in! let me out! game, 107
Letters to the Editor, 34
Life and Times of Che Guevara, 31
lighting
  atmosphere and, 50
  notating, 70
  as part of creative process,
    67
  world and, 54
Liles, William, 116
Lime Kiln Arts, 91
listen and respond around game,
  132
listening
  Active, 127–31
  in brainstorm, 10–11
  to character, 59
  in conflict, 148, 149
  to critique, 140
  games, 89, 131–33
  to radio, 23
  roadblocks to, 131
  to self-talk, 126–27
  total, 131
little black book, 21
Living Stage Theatre Company, 20
Living Theatre, 23, 101, 132
Liz Lerman Dance Exchange, 29, 60,
  80, 102–03
Lloyd, Davidson, 37–38, 77, 80
logic
  central element, 49
  for a character, 43–44, 58
  of a piece, 49
  questions about, 30
  of a world, 54
Long, Andrew, 19, 77
Lord of the Rings, 95

Magritte, René, 56
making an object, 19, 25
mask
    in graphics, 65
    Indonesian, 42
    initial idea, 19–20
    round with, 9
Masterson, John, 133, 135
material, for a piece
    definition of, 28
    generating, 28–39
    physically organizing, 69–74
    shaping, 40–44
    using a file for, 28
    workshopping draft, 74–75
Mather, Jeff, 34
McCain, Tim, 20
mediation, 149
Medicine Show Theatre Ensemble,
    13, 38, 63
meditation, 24, 110
Medoff, Mark, 57
Meisner, Sanford, 132
Mendler, Skip, 18
message. See statement and mission
metaphors
    audience and, 52
    collecting, 33
    movement metaphor, 63
    questions about, 30
Metcalf, C. W., 15, 30, 42, 45, 77, 94,
    118, 139, 140–41
mindful chaos, 39
Mines, Barry, 91
Minor, Hardin, 5
mirror games
    energy mirror, 16
    instant mirror, 118
    leaderless mirror, 16, 117
    oral mirror, 118
    true mirror, 133
mission statement, 36, 51–52
    premise and mission, 52
    questions about, 30
Montanaro, Tony, 3–4, 9, 11, 12, 13,
    14, 36, 65, 109
Morris, Leslie, 18

motivation, 57–58
mouse-in-the-house game, 115
movement
    with breath and music, 18
    circles exercise, 37
    image exercise, 36–37
    as initial idea, 18
    pattern of, 61
    phrase, 63–64
    as research tool, 38
    storytelling through, 35
    to text, 46
    world and, 54
movement metaphor, 63
movies as initial idea, 23
Murdock, Christine, 89, 108
music. See sound
Mysteries, 132
myth, 23, 49, 54

Nagrin, Daniel, 14, 24, 37, 77, 133
Naked and in Love, 37
narrative voice. See point of view
Native American council, 123, 125
negotiation
    in conflict, 149–50
    over objects, 60
Newman, Naomi, 90, 126
No Exit, 47, 51
nominal group technique, 11

object
    becoming an, 51, 136
    creating an imaginary, 15
    as initial idea, 18–19
    making an, 19–20, 25
    negotiation over, 60
    playing with personal, 19
    round with, 9
    unidentified, in blind offer, 136
    use of, in graphics, 65
O'Donnell, Carolyn, 71
Oedipus, 56
ogreship, rotating, 94–96
O'Malley, Marion, 137
OMIMEO Mime Theatre, 5
O'Neal, John, 52, 104

one-element-at-a-time creative pro-
    cess, 29, 45–67
one-element criticism, 141–42
One Sure Thing: A Cabaret on Death,
    73, 85, 88
Open Theatre, The, 13, 73, 132
opposition, 55
organizing material, 69–79
organizing principle, 40–44
outline, 32, 36, 41, 42–44, 69–74

passive aggression, 108–09
Paterson, Doug, 32
Paton, Bob, 23
Paxton, Steve, 119
personal stories
    emotions and, 88
    as research tool, 35
    See also storytelling
phrase
    beat, 66–67
    movement, 53, 63–64
physicalization
    of character, 58–59
    of psychological states, 63
Playback Theatre, 23
playing
    with character, 57
    and creativity, 6–7
    with design in time, 53
    with energy, 15–16, 118–19
    and failure, 5, 6–7
    music, 18
    with object, 18
    roles, in life, 110–13
    with stage areas, 61
    trust games, 119–20
plays
    Children of a Lesser God, 57
    Don't Drop Grandma, 19
    about family farms, 71
    Horsepower, 33
    Letters to the Editor, 34
    Life and Times of Che Guevara, The,
        31
    Mysteries, 132
    Naked and in Love, 37

No Exit, 47, 51
Power Play, 21
    about rape, 35
    rewriting, 22, 75
Romeo and Juliet, 22
Search for Intelligent Life, 8
Serpent, The, 79
Seven Brides for Five Brothers, 5
    structuring, 40–41, 42–43,
        73–75
Tubes, 54
Plexus, Theatre, 19, 21
Poetics, 55
point of view, 35, 57
Pomo Afro Homos, 74–75, 93, 145
power
    covert, 114–15
    definition of, 107
    in a group, 94–104, 107–10, 125
    persuading with, 125
    power plays, 126
    status and, 109
    struggles, 126
Powerplay, 21
power-sharing structures, 94–104
premise and mission, 52
problem solving
    Active Listening for, 127–30
    in conflict, 103, 145–46, 148–49
    questions for, 99, 103
props, 18–20, 65, 67, 70, 77, 78
protagonist and chorus game, 61–62
protean catch game, 6–7
Provisional Theatre, 35, 70, 95, 107
psychiatry, radical, 112, 123, 126
psychology
    of a character, 43–44, 57–61
    of a group, 106–21

questions
    in Active Listening, 128, 129, 130
    clarifying, 10, 130
    for consensus-building, 99
    creativity and, 29–31
    for critique, 140, 141, 142–43
    for evaluation, 137
    to get to the next step, 29–31, 67

questions (*continued*)
  in interviews, 32–33
  in problem-solving, 103

radio as idea source, 23
Ramayana, 54
reading as idea source, 22–23
Reiffel, David, 75, 96–99
relationship
  to audience, 41, 52–53, 54–55
  between art and therapy, 87–88
  blocking and, 61
  character, 61–62
  power, 94–104
  questions about, 30–31
  with self, 126–27
  spatial, 53
repetition games, 132
research, 25, 31–39
"Revelations," 65
rhythm and timing, 64
rhythmic exercise, 16–17
ritual, 23, 55
roadblocks to listening, 131
Road Company, The, 33, 89, 108
Roadside Theater, 53
roles
  in consensus groups, 97–99
  in group maintenance, 133–37
  in groups, 110–13
Romeo and Juliet, 22
rotating ogreship. *See* ogreship
rounds, 9–10, 25
round-table discussion, 21, 25

safety
  fostering, 85–87
  guidelines for, 85–90
  performer, 62
San Francisco Mime Troupe, 31, 101
Sartre, Jean-Paul, 47, 51
Satir, Virginia, 111, 133
scapegoating, 115
Schechner, Richard, 115
Schirle, Joan, 40, 67, 74
Schrader, Connie, 23

Schroeder, Sue, 19, 92
Schwarzman, Mat, 33
Search for Intelligent Life, The, 8
seeing duet, 133
seeing, feeling, thinking response,
  140–41
self-talk, 77, 126–27
sequence of events, 42
Serpent, The, 79
set
  symbolism and, 55
  world and, 54
Seven Brides for Five Brothers, 5
shaping material, 40–44
Shelton Mann, Sara, 78
Sherman, Joanna, 41
Silent Partners, 23
Sills, Paul, 31
site sculpture, 34
site/sight walks, 34–35
sketches
  character, 34
  essential, 33–34
  site sculpture, 34–35
skills
  Active Listening, 127–30
  communication, 125–50
  leading and following, 109–110,
    136
  peaceful conflict resolution,
    145–149
  supportiveness, 136–37
skill work as idea source, 20–21
Skinner, Beth, 58
Skinner, B. F., 54
sound
  aural statement, 65
  character songs, 38
  clarity, 65
  dynamics, 64–65
  idea source, 18, 53, 67, 78
  -and-movement game, 119, 132
  music, 18, 52–53
  notating, 70
  world and, 54
Spolin, Viola, 14, 94, 117

stage
    direction, 61
    focus, 65–66
Stageworks Touring Company, 71, 76
Star Trek, 47, 49
statement
    audience and, 51–53
    central element of composition,
        51–52
    concept, 47–48
    I-feel-, 147–48
    opening, 49, 65
    problem, 130, 148
    questions about, 30, 52
    sequence and, 42
    visual and aural, 65
    you-, 124, 147
statues exercise, 13–14
    evolving, 13
    random, 13–14
Stockley, Rebecca, 14
storyboarding, 73–74
story pulling, 35–36
storytelling
    duet, 118
    genre of, 43
    as idea source, 21, 25
    personal, 35, 88
    about place, 34–35
    through movement, 35
Story Theater, 31
Strimbeck, Leigh, 73, 103–04
Stropnicky, Gerard, 34, 79, 92, 104,
        144
structure
    as central element of composition,
        51
    character development and, 43–44
    dynamics and, 43
    genre and, 41–42
    inventing improvisational, 29
    of myth, dreams, 23
    outlining, 40–41
    of power in a group, 94–104
stuck, what to do when, 76–79
sub-ogre, 95

subtext, emotional, 60
super-ogre, 95
supporting elements of composition,
        54–67
supportiveness
    and creativity, 136
    games for, 136–37
    by listening, 131
surge game, 115
Sweet, Jeffrey, 60
symbols, 30, 54, 55
Synectics, 136

tai chi, 24
Tale of Two Cities, A, 49
talking stick, 125
Teatro Campesino, El, 53, 102
technical theater, 67
Theatre de la Jeune Lune, 103
Theatre of Dreams, 23
Theatre Plexus, 19, 21
theme or topic
    outlining, 32
    questions about, 30
    rounds on, 9–10
therapist, 93, 95, 111, 112, 123, 133,
        146, 149–50
therapy
    conflict and, 150
    difference between art and, 87–
        88
    group, 120, 149
    for individual insight, 110
through lines, 40, 43
time, structuring, 90–94
timing. *See* rhythm and timing
Tolkien, J. R. R., 95
Tomlin, Lily, 8
toning, 92, 132–33
total listening game, 131
TOUCH Mime Theater, xi, 10, 15,
        18, 23, 35, 42, 47, 66, 70, 73,
        76, 77, 79, 81, 89, 90, 91, 92,
        93, 94, 109, 116, 125, 132,
        136, 141
Touchstone Theatre, 19

town meetings, 33
tragedy, 30, 42
Transactional Analysis, 23, 112
travel-as-a-group game, 116
traveling chair, 125
Traveling Jewish Theatre, A, 52–53,
    90, 126
triangles exercise, 109–10
true mirror game, 133
trust
    affirmations and, 142
    breakdown of, 149–50
    -building, 14
    in creative impulses, 3, 5
    games, 119–20
    mediation and, 149
trust circle game, 120
trying anything, 38–39
Tubes, 54
TV as idea source, 23, 54

Uriona, Carlos, 81, 108

Vann, Barbara, 13, 63
videotaping, 73
vision, 104
visual and verbal clarity, 65–66
visual interest, 25
visual statement, 65

Waiting for Godot, 54
Walden Two, 54
Wallace, Shelley, 21, 125

warm-up, 91–92
watching TV, movies, 23
web of composition,
    central elements 47–53
    illustrations, 48, 49
    supporting elements, 54–67
Williams, Eddie, 5
Wizard of Oz, The, 57
Workgroup, the, 37
world
    internal, of a character, 59
    of a piece, 54
    questions about, 30
WOW Café, 5, 157
writing
    from character's point of view, 57,
        76
    collaborative, 74–76
    free-writing, 22
    idea source, 21–22
    rewriting the classics, 22–23
writing it down
    affirmations, 127
    anything that works, 26, 39
    decisions, 29, 94
    dreams, 23
    in a log or journal, 21–22
    after rounds, 10
    while building objects, 20
Wyckoff, Hogie, 112, 126

Yoga, 24
you-statements, 124, 126, 147